SHOWERS
—— of ——
ENLIGHTENMENT

An Outpouring of God's Hidden
Wisdom for the Heart and Mind

RHONDA ADAMS

WESTBOW
P R E S S®
A DIVISION OF THOMAS NELSON
& ZONDERVAN

Scripture taken from the King James Version of the Bible.

WestBow Press books may be ordered through booksellers or by contacting:

WestBow Press
A Division of Thomas Nelson & Zondervan
1663 Liberty Drive
Bloomington, IN 47403
www.westbowpress.com
1 (866) 928-1240

ISBN: 978-1-5127-4358-6 (sc)
ISBN: 978-1-5127-4357-9 (hc)
ISBN: 978-1-5127-4356-2 (e)

Library of Congress Control Number: 2016911122

Print information available on the last page.

WestBow Press rev. date: 7/8/2016

Contents

Preface

After I was saved in the spring of 1999, I was prompted by God to begin reading the Bible. When I did so, the revelations began, my knowledge increased, and my spiritual growth began. It wasn't long after that I experienced a very intense desire from the Holy Spirit to write the revelations He gave me. Every time I read the Scriptures, the desire came. The revelations were small and basic, but they were vital revelations concerning God and salvation. I learned how to use a computer, design a page, and print it. What came forth were one-page brochures with Bible revelations and prayers for salvation, which I handed out to most people I came in contact with. This project became delayed due to some deep purging by God that went on for a couple of years.

After some of the purging took place, I volunteered to teach the adult Bible study class at my church. I was blessed with the opportunity to do so. Again, I received promptings from the Holy Spirit to write down the Bible study revelations and share the knowledge beyond the church classroom. It was during that time I had learned how to make booklets with covers using a computer. I titled them and printed them, but I wasn't sure what to do with them.

God led me to place them at gas stations. I received permission to leave them on the counters of a few gas stations, and people, believers and nonbelievers alike, picked them up. I learned they were all gone within a day or two. One day, as I entered a gas station I had previously visited, I was asked for some writings on some particular subjects.

The public was being touched by the Word of God. As I went out to other towns and cities to display the booklets, I saw that they were welcomed. I was allowed to place them everywhere I went. Actually, there was only one place where a worker told me that religious material was not allowed to be placed in the store, then immediately she said, "but I'll take them." Store workers sometimes moved the displayed candy boxes on the counter tops to make room for the booklets. Praise God! He showed that the public would read them.

There are many books that are being published by those in the body of Christ, about what God is revealing to them, what He's doing for them in their lives, and what He's doing in their ministries. I have loved reading the shared testimonies of brothers and sisters in Christ. And I have also loved their teachings that I have read. Thank God for these shared testimonies, though the Bible needs to be our initial source for learning.

The Holy Spirit revealed something to me as I was leaving church one day, after talking with others about books. Someone said ironically, "All the world needs is yet another book." I understood their point and agreed to some extent. But as I left the church and drove home in my car, the Holy Spirit revealed something to me that helped me renew my thoughts about the subject. He had apparently heard the conversation about books and didn't agree with the statement made about the books, at least concerning His messages. He recalled this subject to me and revealed His will about writing books with gospel messages and testimonies.

My thoughts were apparently not in line with His, therefore He helped me "renew my mind" (Romans 12:2). It was then I clearly understood what His will was on the matter, and why. As I was leaving church that day the Holy Spirit turned my attention to all the books in the world. He then brought my attention to the fact that Satan has his misleading doctrines showing up in books throughout this world to pollute the minds of those who read them, while most people do not understand the Bible with its life saving messages. Those who are enlightened should get their testimonies out into this world, which many are doing. When God revealed this to me, I understood He wants the testimonies and teachings out in this world, however we are able to do so.

Testimonies are a powerful tool for winning souls. Teaching is also a very powerful tool for winning souls, because people can't act upon or respond to what they do not understand. He made a point to redirect the way in which I thought about published books before I even made it home that day. God is in favor of published books with gospel messages. He told Moses and the other biblical authors to write what they knew and had learned from Him. Jeremiah was told to write what he had heard God speak. John was told to write his revelations. Habakkuk was told by God to write his vision.

So let's get the messages, testimonies, and the Word out to encourage, to increase hope, to warn, to enlighten, and to save souls. To God be the glory. He's coming soon!

Introduction

There is such a great joy when experiencing both the manifestation of the Holy Spirit, and revelations of truth that refresh us and enlighten our souls. The touch of the Holy Spirit is beautiful, and there's something so energizing about having the revealed truth of God's Word enter our souls. It's so satisfying and refreshing, and it feeds our souls so we can grow. I love daily revelations!

Revealed truth seems to ignite the spirit within (the inner man). God is truth, and He is our Creator. Truth is what we were created to live in and by. We were not created to live in lies and deception, which the Devil feeds the whole world (Revelation 12:9). Both lies and deception ruin us, but when we receive the Holy Spirit, His truth restores us.

We were created by God to live in and by truth, and that's why our spirits respond the way they do to the enlightenment from God's truth. With the Holy Spirit in the believer, truth is like an ignition switch. It stirs and moves the believer when it enters. I had come to realize that I crave enlightenment from the Lord, and then He revealed something very beneficial to me years ago that satisfied my cravings.

When I was a babe in Christ, I read through the Bible in sections and received bits of revelations. But then the Holy Spirit taught me to study the Scriptures. When I would sit and read the Bible, He'd bring my attention to something within the verses I was reading. He would then lead me to another section of the Bible where something else had been written on that subject. This would be done several times. Each place in the Bible mentioned something slightly different about the subject, which brought much enlightenment. I began receiving much greater insight from the Holy Spirit when I followed His leading and studied in this way. My knowledge in Christ began to increased dramatically. I began to experience what I would call *growth spurts*. This, of course, gave me a desire to read more in the Bible, and more often.

The Holy Spirit taught me to study. He taught me to pull out many verses on a subject as He led me to them, in the very order that He gave them, and carefully meditate on them. It worked! I began to receive larger doses of truth, the Holy Spirit filled me more and more, and taught me more and more. I believe what I was craving was actually the Spirit's presence, which was there when the knowledge came.

If you study God's Word you are in His will, and He will reveal things to you as He opens your understanding. If you obey Him and study to show yourself approved, He will send you revelations. If you have been baptized by the Holy Spirit, He will make the Scriptures come alive for you.

In *Showers of Enlightenment*, you'll find studies on different biblical subjects. Within each study are many passages of Scripture that will help bring enlighten to you, and will show you how to focus on details in Scripture for enlightenment on subjects of which spiritual knowledge may be desired, or perhaps needed.

Chapter 1

Growing in God's Knowledge

After I was born into God's family, I had a significant encounter with God that helped me to realize that He wanted me to put some things in my life aside, read the Bible, and learn about Him. It began with one card, out of a deck of cards.

Before I was saved, I often played the card game called solitaire. One evening, after I received Jesus as my Savior through a TV evangelist, I was playing solitaire on the floor in my living room. I was 29 years of age. During that evening, I began to receive a little desire, and a thought, to read the Bible. The desire and thought kept coming to me. I considered it for a moment and began to wonder, "was it God?" Being aware that it may be God, I said these words out loud, "God, if You want me to read the Bible, let the next card be an ace." Well, I flipped the card over, and yes, it was an ace. It was not only an ace, it was the ace of hearts. When my eyes set on that heart, something amazing happened inside of me.

I'm not sure what it was about that heart (except perhaps as Scripture says in 1 John 4:8, God is love), but when I saw it, my spirit responded with an awareness of God. My communication with God had just begun. It was the first time in my life that—I discerned God. As I stared at the ace of hearts for that very brief moment, I was discerning the prompting that I was receiving and was beginning to put two pieces of that mysterious puzzle together. It was my first spiritual prompting since having become a follower of Jesus Christ. I'd have to say that it is one of the most amazing moments in life when a born again person hears

1

the Father—for the first time. It's just like a small baby, whose vision is not yet fully developed, who hears its mother's voice, recognizes it, and turns its eyes and head to find that voice that is then becoming familiar.

Had God put the ace of hearts there? No, but He did put the desire in me to request the ace at that moment, knowing it was there. I realized that much. He used that moment to communicate to me His desire that I read the Bible. It was a prompting from God. Being one hundred percent convinced, I put the cards away, got some ice tea and cheese nips, walked to the kitchen table, and started reading the Bible. I believe I haven't played solitaire since that evening. I gave it up for God.

Let's read about God's promptings. Throughout the life of a born-again Christian, God will be prompting that person; it's one way He communicates with us. Please note that the words in brackets in scriptural passages aren't in the King James Version; I have placed them there to help readers who might find the KJV a little difficult to understand. In Philippians chapter 2, verse 13, the apostle Paul gives this revelation:

> "For it is God which worketh [works] in you both to
> will and to do of his good pleasure."

Notice what God does with His followers: He "worketh in you both to will and to do of his good pleasure." "To will" means to have in mind, to have a determination, or to desire. It is God that works within us to lead us in thought (have in mind) to do things that please Him, along with a determination, or active energy (desires) to do those things.

If God puts the desire in us to pray for someone, it's His will and is pleasing to Him. If He puts in our hearts and minds to give, that's again His will and pleasure. If God fills us with a desire to do anything, it is His will. Here's an example. I went to college after high school, but did not graduate. Several years have now passed since I first went to college, and I am now enrolled again in college. This decision came from both a prompting, and dreams (visions of the night).

A few years ago, I began to receive dreams that I was in college again. In the dreams I would be walking on the grounds of a college campus on my way to math class, or English class. The college buildings in each dream were different, and all of them were large and beautiful structures. When I would wake, I would think, "How interesting." After about the second dream, I wondered why I was dreaming about being in school again. Dreams like this came several times within about two years.

One day, while waiting in line to pick up one of my children from school, I felt the presence of the Holy Spirit manifest and recall the dreams. I then received His revelation about why I was receiving the dreams. At that moment, it was revealed to me that He was giving me those dreams. He was trying to direct me back to college. It was at that same moment I felt a strong energetic desire well up within me to go back to school. I would not have even considered this a year or more prior, but God had just prompted. The "will and to do of his good pleasure" was then worked in me. I then knew the path to take, and I was suddenly ready to go to school again. I was so excited to go to school, then, but not before. The prompting from God was a thought along with a great joyful desire "to do" what was thought. In this case it was a thought to go to college.

God often prompts us, and it's beneficial when we are able to discern when it's Him. I was once prompted a year in advance to contact someone I had not seen in a while. Within a year, that person passed away. Being a child of God with the message of salvation from sin, I know the prompting was to tell the person about Jesus Christ, and how to be saved. There are reasons behind the promptings. Again, the prompting was a thought accompanied with an energetic desire to contact them. The desires are sometimes stronger than at other times.

I had been diligently prompted by the Holy Spirit in the past to spend time with another person, not knowing the person would soon be leaving this earth. I suppose God prompted me knowing the love I had for that person. Thank You God.

I've been prompted to write many things as He revealed them. I've been prompted to speak out many times, and at other times to be quiet, which has been very challenging. The notable thought here is that God prompts us to do His will. What might He be prompting you to do these days? Ask God to help you to discern His promptings. You can also learn more about God when you take notice of the things He prompts you to do.

The evening I received the thought and desire to read the Bible, when playing solitaire, it was God's prompting. As He worked in me "both to will and to do of his good pleasure," both the desire and thought arose together. If we withdraw from these promptings, we are withdrawing from doing God's will, whether we are aware of it or not.

I learned that it is God's desire for us to read the Bible, study His teachings, and increase in knowledge about Him. All I did was ask him a question out loud that evening, and He answered. We are instructed to do this, in Matthew, chapter 7, verse 7, in which Jesus stated, "Ask, and it shall be given [to] you." I had asked, and He had answered.

When God answered in the way He did, my spirit was slightly stirred, which revealed to me that it was Him. When I realized it was Him, I could then choose to respond, and know what I was responding to. I also realized that He was near me and watching me, His new child. To begin recognizing the voice of the One who has made us is one of the most incredible moments in a person's life.

Once I began to make time to read the Bible daily, giving God hours of my time, He gave me His time. An amazing thing that happened when I did this was that revelations of what I was reading began to come. Another thing that came, as my knowledge increased, were battles for freedom from the areas that the Devil had me bound.

Not long after I started reading the Bible, a couple of gifts of the Holy Spirit mentioned in 1 Corinthians (12:1–11) began to show up. One of them was the "discerning of spirits." To discern means to know. This gift can be compared to when a television station begins to scramble, and the sound and scenes are not clear at all (I have neither cable nor satellite). When the antenna outside is adjusted, suddenly the pictures on the television become very clear, along with the sound. You then see and hear clearly what is happening on the screen.

This is similar to when the gift of discerning of spirits is manifesting in someone. It's like the spiritual antenna is adjusted by the Holy Spirit, and spiritual perception of the spiritual realm becomes very clear. Concerning what is seen and heard in life, and in people, it becomes very clear what spirit is manifesting. The spirits are identified. The spiritual realm is very active with both the spirits of darkness, and the host of God. That gift dramatically changed my life, and it also revealed many answers about life.

Another gift I eventually received was having visions of hell, heaven, judgments, other things, people, and visions of my personal issues that God would help me begin dealing with. I did not realize at the time that God was honoring the time I chose to sit at His feet and learn from Him, but it's very clear to me now. I did His will, and the flow of knowledge and revelations began to come from Him. I had to move into God's will for Him to move. In Galatians, chapter 6, verse 7, it tells us,

> "Be not deceived; God is not mocked: for whatsoever a
> man soweth [sows], that shall he also reap."

We reap the very things we sow. One day, God led me to consider what I was reaping in my life. I thought about it and began to realize what I seemed to be reaping. Then He led me to understand that it indicated what I was sowing. When I began to understand sowing and reaping in that way, I was able to better discern what I was sowing, and in what amounts. As all other teachings from the Holy Spirit, this was a great revelation.

This knowledge applies to more than just finances. This knowledge can also be applied to sowing in our relationships with people, other things in life, or with God. What we put into our relationship with God is what we will get out of it. What we gain in our time of studying God's Word depends upon the effort we put into the study. If we don't study the Bible very much, we won't gain much spiritual knowledge. We have to take the time to be with God if we are to better know Him, and more easily submit to His will.

God sees if you are pursuing Him in His words. What would you like to reap concerning Bible knowledge, and your relationship with your Savior? What you desire to reap is what you should sow into your relationship with God, and in the knowledge of the things of God. Study!

Growing in Knowledge Brings Freedom

It takes growth in knowledge to free us from the shackles of sin. In John, chapter 8, verse 32, Jesus said,

> "And ye shall know the truth, and the truth shall make you free."

Free from what? From being trapped in and serving sin. An amazing fact to know is that truth sets us free. This means we live by accepting lies in our minds, from the Devil (Revelation 12:9), which binds us up in sin. Consider that if truth is what sets us free, which Jesus stated, then it's lies that bind us. God's words and the Holy Spirit reveal truth, which brings freedom.

I clearly recall when Jesus revealed the truth about a fear that I was previously bound in. There was a time in my life when I wouldn't wear red dresses, or any clothes that would possibly draw attention to me, except for occasions such as weddings. I'd dress down, not up, and I would say perhaps a little boyish, in my opinion.

But, one day, as I stood at the doorway to my hallway, the Holy Spirit chose to deal with me about that issue. First, He brought my attention to the fact that I was insecure about wearing nice dress clothes. My thoughts were then focused on that issue. He then brought to mind words that had been spoken to me in the past about the way I dressed. It wasn't necessarily evil speaking, but rather the way in which the words were spoken to me. As I thought about it, the Holy Spirit revealed how that affected me.

At that moment, when the Holy Spirit led me to consider this, it was revealed to me that I had a *fear*. A *fear* was then identified. The fear was of dressing nicely in public with the possibility of drawing—*negative attention*. It was then He revealed to me—"it's a lie." I had believed the lie that everyone would respond in a *negative* way about the way I dressed, as someone had done in the past. I'd carried that lie around in my mind for years, which affected the way I dressed, in a bad way.

At that moment, my understanding was opened, truth was revealed, and the lie was exposed. At that very moment I became free from a fear that I didn't know I had. I was bound by a lie, which invited a fear. But Jesus knew, and that day He chose to expose the lie and reveal to me what was truth. He led me to freedom, using truth.

Because I chose to follow Jesus, study, and began to do what I learned, He was doing what He said He would do. Jesus came to preach deliverance to the captives (Luke 4:18). I'd been held captive by a lie, but after Jesus revealed the truth, I was released from Satan's captivity. The Bible reveals that the Devil is the father of all lies (John 8:44), and there are many we carry around with us without realizing it.

God's words are filled with the truth that we need for freedom from fears, angers, addictions, and so forth. Again, verse 32 states, "know the truth," because knowing truth "shall make you free." God's truth is available and is in the Bible, but we need to study it.

Chapter 7 includes a testimony I have given of how God helped me become free from the addiction of tobacco by revealing thoughts of truth in the midst of the battle. Revealed truth is very powerful; it can indeed set us free. In this world there are many battles we encounter, and there are many different ways in which we try to deal with them. Truth, though, is a powerful weapon to use. Consider that if truth sets us free, then truth is what breaks or loosens the shackles. When this happens, we become changed. Truth exists, but we have to know it. Jesus will reveal it as we grow in His knowledge, so study the Scriptures daily. Also, pray that He will guide you through them in your study.

God Wants to Teach Us

God has so much He desires to teach us from His Bible, and if we take the time to study, the Teacher (the Holy Spirit) will show up to teach. He's waiting on us. This is stated in John, chapter 14, verse 26, in which Jesus told His followers,

> "But the Comforter, which is the Holy Ghost, whom the Father will send in my name, he shall teach you all things, and bring all things to your remembrance, whatsoever I have said unto you."

When we receive the Holy Spirit, we not only receive the Comforter, but a teacher also. He will "teach you all things," He says. He will teach us everything we need to know, and what we want to know. Ask Him many things. Ask Him, "Lord, what do You know about this (or that) that You can teach me?" "Lord, how do I accomplish this (or that)?" "Lord, why do I do these things?" "Lord, why do they do those things that they do?" "Lord, what have You called me to do in my life?" "Lord, what determines what gifts Your people receive?" This is asking for wisdom, which He gives.

The Holy Spirit is the Teacher of His Word. What we have to do is give Him our time, and His revelations will come. Isn't that amazing to know? Truth is that Satan deceives and destroys his children, but God loves, educates, and trains up His children. Hallelujah! Satan hides both himself and knowledge from his children, but God reveals Himself to, and increases knowledge in, those who follow Him.

If you read in Matthew, chapter 5, verse 2, chapter 7, verse 29, chapter 9, verse 35, and chapter 11, verse 1, you will see again and again that Jesus taught people while He was here. These are only a few verses that reveal He was, and is, a teacher. In Hebrews, chapter 13, verse 8, it tells us,

> "Jesus Christ the same yesterday, and to day, and for ever."

According to this verse, Jesus *never* changes. He will always be the same. Jesus taught them then and He teaches us today, because He is exactly the same today as He was then. He wanted people taught then, and He wants us taught today. The way in which He taught Paul, Peter, and John is the exact same way in which He teaches us today. Referring back to John, chapter 14, verse 26, it reveals another very important thing that the Holy Spirit does for us. The Holy Spirit will:

> "bring all things to your remembrance, whatsoever I [Jesus] have said unto you."

Notice here that Jesus told His followers that the Holy Spirit, when He was to be sent, was going to bring to their memory (recall) things that He had spoken to them. He recalls information. Not only does the Holy Spirit teach us, you can expect Him to bring to mind needed information, or whatever He has spoken to you in times past.

When a vision you've had in the past comes to mind, the Holy Spirit is recalling it. If something you've learned previously from the Holy Spirit comes to mind, it is the Holy Spirit recalling it. It's not you recalling, but Him fulfilling this verse. He says He'll bring it to your mind. As I was leaving church one day, the Holy Spirit recalled these words to me, "be ye therefore wise as serpents, and harmless as doves" (Matthew 10:16). The Holy Spirit has often recalled these words to me through the years, to consider and act upon it at different times.

Read, Feed, and Grow

Does God want us all to learn and grow in His knowledge, or just the pastors, teachers, and evangelists? All of us. In 2 Peter, chapter 3, verse 18, the believers are told,

> "But grow in grace, and in the knowledge of our Lord
> and Savior Jesus Christ."

We are all instructed to "grow" in knowledge about Jesus. We all have purposes to fulfill in our lives. God wants His children to learn His words and grow in spiritual knowledge. If a person comes to Christ and does not constantly read and fill himself, or herself with the word of God, the spiritual growth will be hindered, and so will freedoms. In 2 Timothy, chapter 2, verse 15, it says,

> "Study to shew [show] thyself approved unto God,
> a workman that needeth [needs] not to be ashamed,
> rightly dividing the word of truth."

Paul told Timothy, his brother in Christ, to study. The word "study" means making an effort, to be earnest, or diligent. We have to make the effort to know God's Word, to be able to live by it and teach what we know. The reason given was, "to shew thyself approved unto God." When we study, and God sees if we do, we're are showing that we are looking for His knowledge, and He approves of the effort given. God then brings the knowledge to us so that we are able to rightly divide the word of truth. Read in Acts chapter 8, verses 26-31, where it reveals that God saw a eunuch trying to understand the Scriptures. He then sent a man with knowledge of the Scriptures to help him understand what he was reading. God saw his effort, responded to it, and helped him.

"Rightly diving" is from the Greek word *orthotomeo,* which means to make a straight cut. *Ortho* means *straight,* and *temno,* from which *tomeo* comes from, means to *cut.* An example given for the meaning of this word is to dissect something. It's a careful cut and division for examining and studying. Trying to simply explain this, "rightly dividing the word of truth" means to open up the Word of God and very carefully study to discern Scripture, so that it is understood and taught correctly. God would like us to rise to a level of understanding where we can not only live by it, but effectively explain the Scriptures to others who are in need of understanding. With the leading of the Holy Spirit, and much study, this can be done.

The baptism of the Holy Spirit is necessary to understand the things of God, because, as Scripture states, no one can understand the things of God except God Himself (1 Corinthians 2:11). Therefore, the Spirit of God has to be received to be able to understand things pertaining to Him. God's will is for us to learn about Him. In 1 Peter, chapter 2, verses 1–2, we are given this about spiritual growth,

> "Wherefore laying aside all malice, and all guile, and hypocrisies, and envies, and all evil speakings,"

> "As newborn babes, desire the sincere milk of the word, that ye may grow thereby."

A newborn baby sounds the alarm (cries, or whimpers) when a feeding is needed. When there is a lack of feeling full in the belly of the baby (adults also), it brings discomfort. When the discomfort is felt, the alarm (cries) begins to sound. Feeling full brings satisfaction and comfort to the body. Correct? As babes desire their food for filling, which is milk, the Word of God should also be desired by those born into God's family, "as newborn babes." The desire draws us to the Word so that we can feed off of it (take it in), get a filling of the Spirit, experience the satisfaction and comfort of it, and "grow."

God wants the babes to grow in knowledge and maturity, and that is why He prompts us to read the Bible and study. Make time to sit with the Holy Spirit daily and study. He desires this.

One of the blessings of growing in the knowledge of the Word of God is coming to maturity in Christ, being skillful in the Word, and having the ability to discern good from evil. This, in turn, helps us to live a better life. Hebrews, chapter 5, verses 13–14 teach on this, saying,

> "For everyone that useth [uses] milk is unskilful in the word of righteousness: for he is a babe."

> "But strong meat belongeth [belongs] to them that are of full age, even those who by reason of use have their senses exercised to discern both good and evil."

"Full age" in this verse means to be grown, or complete, both mentally and morally. Being "unskilful in the word" is an indication of being on milk. At this stage, we are classified as babes in Christ and in need of growth. But when we become skillful in the Word of God, we then become those who are mature, and

> "by reason of use have their [our] senses exercised."

Having the "senses exercised" means the spiritual senses are trained. The word "senses" is from the Greek word *aistheterion,* which is the organ, or power, of perception. When we begin to use the eyes and ears of the spirit, mixed with the knowledge that God provides, we are exercising the senses and preparing to move from the milk to the meat. God will then take us out of the high chair and let us sit at the table. When the spiritual perception becomes sharpened, we are growing to a mature level at which we are more able to be used for the work of God.

The skillful children of God are those who make "use" of the Word of God, through practice. Use what you have learned. Practice it. It is God's will for us take action and do what we learn in Christ. Like anything else in life, we become good at what we practice.

Do What You Learn

It's very easy to sit back and allow the teachers, pastors, evangelists, and so forth, to be the spiritual leaders they are, doing much spiritual work for the Lord. But spiritual growth and labor in the Lord is not only for them. We all have a responsibility to learn and grow. The leaders are here to teach the unlearned until they grow and apply it. Let's look at James, chapter 1, verses 22–25, which makes this clear, saying,

> "But be ye doers of the word, and not hearers only, deceiving your own selves."

> "For if any be a hearer of the word, and not a doer, he is like unto a man beholding his natural face in a glass [mirror]:"

> "For he beholdeth [beholds] himself, and goeth [goes] his way, and straightway forgetteth [forgets] what manner of man he was."

> "But whoso looketh [looks] into the perfect law of liberty, and continueth [continues] therein, he being not a forgetful hearer, but a doer of the work, this man shall be blessed in his deed."

Looking back in verse 22, we are instructed to, "be ye doers of the word, and not hearers only." We can understand from these words that doing what's written in the Bible is God's will for us. God wants hearers who become doers. Consider this simple thought of comparison. What if you told your child to take out the trash, the child hears and knows your will, but it doesn't get done? What if you told your child to clean his or her room (or some other task), he or she hears and knows your request, but it doesn't get done? This is actually a case of hearing and not doing. Wouldn't you love for your child to be ready and willing to quickly move at your requests? God desires this from His children as well. Only hearing the Word of God as preachers preach and teachers teach is not God's will.

Verse 22 warns that hearing only and not acting on what is heard or learned is "deceiving your own selves." If we accept the thought that we can hear the will of God, take it lightly and not apply it, deception is creeping in. In John, chapter 14, verse 21, Jesus said, "He that hath my commandments, and keepeth them, he it is that loveth me." Again, we see here that it's not only having the commandments, but keeping (doing) them is what expresses a love towards Jesus. We can't just have a Bible, we have to learn it and live it. We need to have hearts that are willing to practice what is learned, which is pleasing to God. That is what He will bless. Looking back into verses 23–24, it tells us what being one who only hears is compared to:

> "For if any be a hearer of the word, and not a doer, he is like unto a man beholding his natural face in a glass:"

> "For he beholdeth himself, and goeth his way, and straightway forgetteth what manner of man he was."

To hear the Word of God and not learn to live by it is compared to a person looking into a mirror, which is the meaning of the word "glass" in verse 23. The Holy Spirit caught my attention with this example given. After I thought about it, I went in front of my bathroom mirror, which is on a wall, and looked at my face. I observed just about all my facial features for about one minute, then I stepped aside to the right of the mirror. Amazingly, most of the details I had just looked at were forgotten. Well, I tried it again. I stood in front of the mirror one more time, looked at my features, and stepped aside from the mirror. Most of what I observed was immediately forgotten, again.

To give a little more understanding about the reality of this truth, I'll share what God has recently revealed to me concerning this. I've witnessed instructions and commands that had been given to some people, and the instructions were not immediately carried out. Later, it was stated by the one who did not immediately carry out the task, "O, I forgot." As my ears heard the word "forgot," God recalled these words to me, "forgetful hearer." The task was not immediately carried out, therefore, they "straightway forgetteth," or quickly forgot to do what they heard they were suppose to do. They heard, was not a doer, and forgot.

The message in this is that if a person hears or reads the messages from the Bible and does not receive understanding and apply the teachings, the messages will be quickly forgotten. God does not desire this from us. We need to take action and do it. We've got this one life to choose God and His will, and do His will. In verse 25, we are reminded of the blessings of not forgetting, but doing the will of God:

> "But whoso looketh into the perfect law of liberty, and continueth [continues] therein, he being not a forgetful hearer, but a doer of the work, this man shall be blessed in his deed."

Notice who will be "blessed in his deed." "Not a forgetful hearer, but a doer of the work." According to this verse, God is going to bless the person doing what they learn from the Scriptures. Those who forget will not be blessed in his deeds. So, do what you learn, because God will bless your deeds. Being doers of His work makes us skillful in the Word, and no longer babes in Christ. We will be better teachers, or whatever God calls us to do in His service, when we make use of His Word. James also made it a point to mention that continuing in the Word is necessary.

Hosea, chapter 4, verse 6, reveals the seriousness of not taking God's knowledge to heart and acting upon it. It confirms, with detail, what was just read in James (1:22–25). Here is what God said about His people Israel while in their rebellion:

> "My people are destroyed for lack of knowledge: because thou hast [you have] rejected knowledge, I

will also reject thee, that thou shalt [shall] be no priest
to me: seeing thou hast forgotten the law of thy God, I
will also forget thy [your] children."

Notice what we are given here as a reason for the people of God
being destroyed—their "lack of knowledge." The Israelites were swept
off their land by their enemies due to rebellion. They lost what God had
given them, which was a land of their own to live in, along with God's
righteous rules that would bring blessings to the people and the land.
Another part of this verse that brings enlightenment is where God said,

"because thou hast rejected knowledge, I will also reject
thee"

Do you see the danger in rejecting the Word of God? In their
rebellion there was a rejection of God's knowledge. It's not that God's
Word wasn't sent to the people in the nation, because it was. It was
rejected by them. God's knowledge was sent through the mouths of
prophets (men of God). The people in the nation saw not a prophet,
but mere men, and didn't care for the words they spoke, which were
words directly from God Himself.

We can observe among us today a rejection of God and His Word.
It's not that it isn't being preached, taught, and proclaimed in this
generation, because it is. There is a lack of interest in the knowledge of
God by most in this generation (not all). Consider the fact that the word
reject means: refusing to accept, refuse to consider, refuse to submit to,
refuse to hear, or to throw out as if useless. Doesn't this shine a little
light on how to recognize who is rejecting God's Word? If someone
refuses to considered it, it is being rejected. If it is being refused to be
heard, it is being rejected. If it is deemed by anyone to be useless, it is
being rejected. Also, if it is being refused to be submitted to, that is a
rejection.

When the Israelites rejected knowledge given, God said, "I will also
reject thee." They reaped what they sowed—rejection. Also note that
in Matthew, chapter 10, verse 33, Jesus also said that He would deny
those who deny Him. We reap what we sow.

There is a little more to look at in this verse to help shape a good message about the danger of neglecting God's Word. This part of the verse reinforces the message in James, chapter 1, verse 24, about forgetting the Word of God. After God said He'd reject His people, He further said,

"seeing thou hast forgotten the law of thy God."

They forgot the laws of God, which was part of their troubles. It is clear that there is a danger in rejecting the teachings of the Bible, the Word of God. If the Word of God is rejected, God is being rejected. We are to be doers of the Word, not forgetful hearers. We have been given by God both His Word of knowledge, and His Holy Spirit, to help us learn and do His will under the new covenant with Jesus Christ. The Word of God has life-changing power and it should not be taken lightly, nor neglected.

There is an unseen enemy that seeks to destroy us, and we need God's wisdom to know how to put up a defense against him. The Devil has snares, weapons, and traps, but the Word of God is part of our armor. It is the sword of the Spirit. In 1 Peter, chapter 5, verse 8, it states,

"Be sober, be vigilant; because your adversary the devil,
as a roaring lion, walketh [walks] about, seeking whom
he may devour."

According to this verse, the Devil is walking around and he's looking to see whom he will be able to destroy, or as Scripture says, "devour." Knowledge of God is what will help us be victorious over the battles we face in life, especially in these last days.

Ask God for Knowledge and Wisdom

"If any of you lack wisdom, let him ask of God, that
giveth [gives] to all men liberally, and upbraideth not;
and it shall be given him."

"But let him ask in faith."

This is written in James, chapter 1, verses 5–6. The conditions to getting some of God's wisdom, according to this verse, is only to ask Him. Wow! How awesome it is to know this, and to be able to share it with others who may not know. God will give us His wisdom "liberally," which means plentifully, or freely. The One who created, by His knowledge, the heavens, the earth, and all that exists, shares His knowledge with anyone who desires it and asks for it. "But let him ask in faith" it says. When you ask God for His wisdom in anything, expect it to come. When you ask God for knowledge about something and wait for the knowledge to be revealed, that is asking in faith. When the knowledge begins to manifest, it is God fulfilling His Word, and your request. Always give Him thanks. Praise God!

Matthew, chapter 22, verse 29, offers us something very enlightening about the result of not knowing Scripture. Knowing the Scriptures well is very beneficial. Some Sadducees were asking about marriage in heaven, and Jesus answered them beginning with these words,

"Ye do err, not knowing the scriptures, nor the power of God."

To "err" means to roam, wander away, or to stray. Jesus revealed that their erring was due to "not knowing the scriptures." This statement He made exposes the reason that we stray from God, which is "not knowing the Scriptures." Invest plenty of time in studying the Scriptures. God will bless your effort, and understanding will come from Him. He's always available to teach, and we need to discipline ourselves to daily take in the Word.

Unbelievers do not know what's in the Scriptures and are thus far from God. Consider that when you are far enough from someone, you can't hear them when they speak. We can say that if we have wandered from God, it's difficult to hear Him. Under the old covenant, the Israelites rejected knowledge and were distant from God. When I was roaming around in this world in sin, I didn't know what was written in the Scriptures and was distant from God. Increased knowledge of the Scriptures helps in preventing us from straying.

Before I was purged, I was definitely not walking anywhere near the righteous path of life. When Scripture began to come alive to me, as the Holy Spirit began revealing its truth, my walk slowly became straightened. That's when I began to see the path of life that God wanted me on, and it truly was good to see. My erring has been corrected by knowing what is in the Scriptures, and still is today. The Scriptures are a guide for us, if we accept them and do what is written.

Just as when a sheep errs, when it wanders away from the flock, the shepherd will search for that sheep and bring it back to the flock. Well, the Holy Spirit, along with the Word of God (our shepherd), leads us to the righteous path in life. God's flock is moving in the direction of eternity with Him, and He doesn't want any of us straying from where the others in the flock are going. Our focus should be the path of righteousness.

This brings my thoughts to my pet chicken. My family has experienced quite a bit of drama since I began raising chickens. I have found that many animals in town want to eat or harass my chickens, and snakes want their eggs. We live near fields of sugar cane, beans, corn, and cotton. At this time, I've lost all but one chicken and she's my pet. We no longer have a rooster which would watch over the hens to keep them gathered and protected, like a shepherd. They would usually stay gathered under trees, or other coverings we have in the yard. Being alone, my hen has sometimes roamed around our large yard carelessly in search of bugs. When she does this, she is vulnerable to attacks from the chicken hawk, her enemy.

The chicken hawk flies overhead daily in search of what it will devour for the day. The ways of the chicken hawk can be compared to the ways of the Devil, who "walketh about, seeking whom he may devour" (1 Peter 5:8). Our protection from the roaming Devil is in knowing and doing the Word of God. It provides a covering. Doing what God says to do will keep us from erring from Him, and under protection. But praise God! If we fall and stumble along the way, He will counsel us, guide us, and give us His wisdom to make our way back to Him. He desires not to lose us, but to keep us.

God Tells Us to Gain Wisdom

Do you know that God wants us to be wise? Yes He does. In Proverbs, chapter 4, verses 7–8, it says this:

> "Wisdom is the principal thing; therefore get wisdom: and with all thy getting get understanding."

> "Exalt her, and she shall promote thee: she shall bring thee to honour, when thou dost [you do] embrace her."

In verse 7, what is stated as being the "principal thing," meaning the first or most important thing? The answer given is, "wisdom." Gaining wisdom should be a priority for the born-again Christian. When I think back to when I lived without Jesus in my life, and lacking His wisdom, I certainly reaped the consequences. From heaven's view, I know it was not looking good for me, but God pulled me out of the whirlpool of sin and is blessing me with His wisdom, which I welcome.

In verse 8 it says that wisdom "shall promote thee," if you exalt it. Doesn't that sound attractive? To exalt means to raise up, lift, or glorify. To promote means to advance in rank. Learn to lift the Word of God above all in your life; His wisdom will promote you. If you read of Daniel in the Old Testament, you will see that he was promoted to very high positions. He gained much wisdom in his life, from God that is.

Wisdom will also bring honor to the one who embraces it. God's wisdom is free, and there is no given limit to the amount we can seek Him for. We can dip into the Bible everyday and pull out some hidden wisdom. Not one time I have ever received from God, "That's enough, close the book." As I would read until one or two in the morning, He was still there teaching and revealing. He never sleeps. Actually, He will continually prompt us to study the Scriptures and grow in knowledge.

I recall going through a Bible study of Ecclesiastes for Bible classes on Sundays in the past. I went through every verse researching words in Hebrew to get the clearest meaning I could from the Holy Spirit, to bring fresh new insight in any area of the study I was able to. Towards the end of studying this book of the Bible, the Holy Spirit began to open my understanding about the subject of wisdom that I had not comprehended throughout most of the study.

All Solomon [son of King David] did was ask for wisdom, and God freely poured it upon him. "For he was wiser than all men," 1 Kings, chapter 4, verse 31 says. God gave him an amount of wisdom that exceeded the wisdom of all others. People and kings of other nations journeyed to his kingdom to hear the wisdom that came out of his mouth.

His wisdom came from the same God who tells us to ask Him for wisdom. There is only one requirement, which is—ask Him. I challenge you to ask Him. Wisdom will teach you to speak better, act better, live better, raise your children better, manage your finances better, and honor God better.

The verse above says that "she [wisdom] shall bring thee to honour," and our part is only to embrace it. So, we should seek God for wisdom and hold firmly to it throughout life. I have actually hugged my Bible in one of those good Holy Spirit filled moments, though that isn't what this verse actually means.

Beware, however, some wisdom is of this world and not of God. In 1 Corinthians, chapter 2, verses 6–7, the apostle Paul wrote,

> "Howbeit we speak wisdom among them that are perfect [mature]: yet not the wisdom of this world, nor of the princes of this world, that come to nought [nothing]:"

> "But we speak the wisdom of God in a mystery, even the hidden wisdom, which God ordained before the world unto our glory:"

Paul mentioned in verse 6, "wisdom of this world," and in verse 7 he mentioned the "wisdom of God." This shows us that wisdom can be gained from either of two places: the heavenly realm, or the earthly realm. In verse 7 it reveals that God's wisdom is the "hidden wisdom." There are things in life that mankind cannot figure out, because God has hidden much wisdom about it. However, God has given His children access to the hidden wisdom (Matthew 13:11). Solomon was given the hidden wisdom. Consider what is written in 1 Corinthians, chapter 3, verse 19, which says,

"For the wisdom of this world is foolishness with God."

This is interesting to know and something we should keep in mind. The wisdom that is received in this world's system is foolishness to God. We grow up in this world being filled with its foolish wisdom. God calls us to Him to begin instilling His wisdom. Once we begin to grow in God's wisdom, we then begin to get glimpses of the foolishness God sees in this world. God's wisdom is mysterious truth, and the world, whose god is Satan, lacks this truth. God wants His children taught in and led by His truth, which He freely gives.

God will always teach us something new if we give Him our time. In what is believed by many to be the last generation before the second coming of Jesus Christ, we have the opportunity to be a part of learning and proclaiming God's wisdom to the ends of the earth, and then the end will come (Matthew 24:14). The lost souls need to hear what we have heard and believed. John wrote about this end-time generation, and we're seeing it being fulfilled. Let us not be idle servants but reading, studying, and growing in God's knowledge. We need to then pass it on. Just think, the King of heaven wants to spend time with you, and teach you what He knows.

Please pray for those who don't have a Bible, such as those in other countries, and that they will receive one to read and learn. Pray for the protection of brothers and sisters in Christ who would perhaps be in danger if they had one in their possession. I know they would be grateful if we would think of them often and keep them in our prayers.

Prayer for Wisdom

Lord, I thank You for salvation through Jesus Christ, Your Son. Your
Word says that if we ask anything according to Your will,
You hear us. Your Word also says all we have to do to gain wisdom is
to ask You for it. Will You increase my knowledge and wisdom
as I read and study Your Word? Teach me what I need to know about
You, Your will for me, and Your kingdom. Teach me to think,
speak, and live in wisdom, that I might be a vessel of honor for Your glory.
Help me apply Your wisdom in all areas of my life, that I may be a
light in honor of You. For this, I thank You. In Jesus' name I pray, amen.

Chapter 2

God Mysteriously Searches Hearts

What if you knew if the Spirit who in the beginning said, "Let there be light," the Spirit who parted the Red Sea for Moses, who spoke with Job, flooded the entire world in the days of Noah, confused the languages at Babel, ordered the annihilation of Sodom and Gomorrah, who is the God of Abraham, Isaac, and Jacob, was going to come and search your heart and thoughts today, to see what is in there?

I was very enlightened when I realized God was often searching my mind and heart when I wasn't even aware of it. I love searching for God in the events recorded in Scripture, and at some point I began to understand that He is very interested in searching us too. One day, I realized He comes to search and know what is in my heart, while there is no manifestation of His presence.

In this chapter, I write about God searching the hearts of humanity, including how, why, and when He may do so. Many Scriptures that reveal someone's heart being searched by God are given in this chapter. I have pulled out details from these verses to reveal God behind the scenes in these verses. This is a close-up look at the Creator, the Spirit behind the Scriptures, so we can understand a little more about Him, and His never-ending interest in our hearts. Knowing these things helps us to know Him.

Where Do Thoughts Come From?

We will be focusing on the hearts not as the the physical organ but as the center of our being, our spirit. Scripture reveals that the spirit is what gives us life, the body does not (John 6:63; James 2:26). The body is only a vessel for the spirit to dwell in. Here are some verses that reveal how your thoughts, your spirit, and your heart are all connected. Let's begin with Isaiah, chapter 55, verses 8-9, in which God said this about humanity,

> "For my thoughts are not your thoughts, neither are your ways my ways, saith the Lord."

> "For as the heavens are higher than the earth, so are my ways higher than your ways, and my thoughts than your thoughts."

I want to pull out a small section from these verses to focus on. If you will notice within these two verses God said of Himself, "my thoughts." God thinks. To this we'll add knowledge given in John, chapter 4, verse 24, in which it states this about God:

> "God is a Spirit."

This is all we'll pull out of this verse. "God is a Spirit," and as we just read, He has thoughts. Now consider that if God is a Spirit, having no form or body, and He thinks, then we can conclude that—spirits think. It is the spirit of man that thinks.

Consider that when the spirit departs from the body at death, the body no longer thinks, because the spirit is gone. When the spirit departs from the body, the thoughts and the knowledge it has go with it, as seen in the parable that Jesus gave of the rich man and Lazarus (Luke 16:19–31). This is also indicated in Revelation, chapter 6, verses 9–11. The point to be made, or knowledge to be gained, is that our spirit is the very center of our being. When "thought of the heart" is mentioned in the Bible, the spirit is involved because the spirit thinks.

When the word "heart" is used in these instances, it refers to the spirit of man, also known as the inner man.

Jesus taught that what was in the mind was also in the heart, and what was in the heart was in the mind, because they're connected. In Matthew, chapter 9, the connection between the two is clearly revealed. In this verse Jesus was speaking to some scribes who didn't like hearing Him forgive people's sins. In Matthew, chapter 9, verse 4, we read,

> "And Jesus knowing their thoughts said, Wherefore think ye evil in your hearts?"

Notice Jesus said their thinking was, "in your hearts." Look at His words this way, "Wherefore think…in your hearts?" Our thoughts are connected with what is in our hearts. They are actually manifestations of what's in our hearts. What arises in thought comes forth from the heart, the inner man.

Let's look at some issues, or sins, that come up and out from the heart into the thoughts. In Mark, chapter 7, verses 20–23, Jesus gave a list of sins and revealed where they come from. Verses 20–23 state,

> "And he [Jesus] said, That which cometh out of the man, that defileth the man."

> "For from within, out of the heart of men, proceed evil thoughts, adulteries, fornications, murders,"

> "Thefts, covetousness, wickedness, deceit, lasciviousness, an evil eye, blasphemy, pride, foolishness:"

> "All these evil things come from within, and defile the man."

Looking back at verse 21, Jesus clearly stated that "out of the heart… proceed evil thoughts." Again, it is mentioned that the thoughts come out of the heart, and this is the area that Jesus searches. These issues are what make humanity unholy in the ears and eyes of God. According to Jesus, the mystery behind this behavior is that the sins are committed because the thoughts to do them are there first. The thoughts are corrupted, therefore the actions, or behavior, that follow are corrupted. If the thoughts of sin are removed, the sins will then be removed also. View Jesus' words in this way:

- adultery is in the thoughts
- fornication is in the thoughts
- murder is in the thoughts
- theft is in the thoughts
- covetousness is in the thoughts
- wickedness is in the thoughts
- deceit is in the thoughts
- lasciviousness (lustful desires) is in the thoughts
- an evil eye is in the thoughts
- blasphemy is in the thoughts
- pride is in the thoughts
- foolishness is in the thoughts

All these sins stem from the thoughts of people. The actions of these sins come forth due to the thoughts being there first. These sins are in the minds of people generation after generation. If the sin is in the mind it's in the heart, the area Jesus searches. God tells us to change our thoughts using His Word, which will cleanse our hearts. As our thoughts change, so also will our ways. If we desire to change, we need to change the way in which we think. An amazing fact to know is that we can actually change and control the way we think, says God. He instructs us to do so.

Jesus Searches Your Thoughts

"I am he which searcheth the reins [the minds] and hearts: and I will give unto every one of you according to your works."

These are the words of Jesus written in Revelation, chapter 2, verse 23. According to what is read here, where does Jesus search? He "seacheth the reins and hearts." Note the present tense of "searcheth," which means He searches. The word "reins" means the mind. Jesus looks into both our hearts, and our minds (thoughts). Jesus often referred to the 'thought of the heart,' which reveals they are connected.

Scripture reveals that God has been searching hearts throughout generations, and still does today. John, who wrote the book of Revelation, received these revelations from Jesus well after He had died on the cross. But the fact that God searches hearts was revealed also in the Old Testament days, by the Lord, which reveals that God has been searching minds and hearts since the beginning. This will be seen in upcoming Scriptures. In Jeremiah, chapter 11, verse 20, it says,

> "But, O Lord of hosts, that judgest [judges] righteously,
> that triest [try] the reins and the heart"

This passage from the Old Testament reveals that it was then known by some that God tries, or tests, the minds and hearts of humanity. He has been doing this since before Jesus came as our Savior. But God is not done yet with His searching. He continues to search in the hearts and minds of the people in this generation. Jeremiah, chapter 17, verse 10, says of God,

> "I the Lord search the heart, I try the reins, even to give
> every man according to his ways, and according to the
> fruit of his doings."

If you will note that the words of God are saying "I...search." Again, notice the indication is present tense. It means "daily searching." Among all things that God does, one thing we can be sure of is that He searches our hearts. According to this verse, one purpose for His searching is to know of our ways, and give to each of us according to our ways. This was also stated by Jesus in the verse previously given, "I will give unto every one of you according your works" (Revelation 2:23). So, if our works, or doings, are good, then we will receive good from the Lord. Also, as God leads us to change for good, we know that He is leading us into good rewards that are to come.

God Searched Hearts before the Flood

If we look into the Scriptures that describe what took place before the flood of Noah's days, there is evidence that God took the time to search the hearts and minds of all the people before the judgment came. In the Scriptures, God actually reveals what the condition of their hearts was, which was not good at all.

In Genesis, chapter 6, verse 1, it says that "men began to multiply on the face of the earth, and daughters were born unto them." In verse 2 we find that "the sons of God" chose themselves wives that were not followers of God. Some believe this to be wicked angels that joined with mortal women in marriage, and had children with them.

God then reveals in verse 3 that He will not always strive with mankind. In the Hebrew text it actually states that He will not always strive with man in their straying, or erring. Also, it seems that in those days God declared a shorter lifespan—120 years—for humanity. Some believe this means God gave that generation 120 years to repent before the flood was to occur. Verse 4 mentions giants (nephilim) being on earth, and the unequally yoked marriages that produced children. Then we have verse 5 which contains the information we are looking for about the hearts of men. It states,

> "And God saw that the wickedness of man was great in
> the earth, and that every imagination of the thoughts
> of his heart was only evil continually."

When we divide this in sections to meditate on, we can form a better picture of what was taking place concerning the ways of the people in the generation before the flood. Where it reads, "And God saw that the wickedness of man [mankind] was great in the earth," there are a few things to take notice of. God looks at the earth from heaven. Not only did He then see the wickedness of the people, but also, "the thoughts of his [their] heart." Here we see where God revealed that He knew what was in the hearts of the people living during that time. He not only saw the outward wickedness, He looked inside at their hearts and minds and knew "every imagination of the [their] thoughts." He knew all that was in their thoughts. How? It is the area He searches.

To go a little deeper in thought and understanding about this, it helps to know what the word search means. To search means to look through, to seek, or to probe. To probe means to examine thoroughly. In His search (probing) of hearts, God found one heart to be righteous—the heart of Noah. Consider that if only one man was found to be righteous, then we can understand that God went throughout the land, house to house, tent to tent, and cave to cave *searching* each one of those hearts before the flood.

According to God, their thoughts were "only evil continually." In the Hebrew text it states that their thinking was only evil, all day long. According to what has been given, there wasn't one part of the day that evil wasn't present in their minds. All thoughts that surfaced were deemed by God to be evil. This information exposes what was going on in the minds of men and women at that time. They had thoughts of violence and corruption (Genesis 6:11) all day.

Proverbs, chapter 23, verse 7, reveals this about humanity, "For as he thinketh in his heart, so is he." We only act out the way in which we think. If the thoughts are evil, the actions will be also. As they thought in their heart, so were they. This is why God teaches us to think righteously, because righteous actions will then follow.

Scripture reveals that when a land becomes filled with sin, judgment follows. But, we can know that a search of the hearts will be made first. Abraham was told by God that his descendants would come out of a judged nation (Egypt) and go into the Promised Land when the sins of the Amorites were full (Genesis 15:14-16). God was awaiting the time the land of the Amorites would be saturated with sin, which would be their time for judgment. God knew their hearts.

We can see evidence of this also in the case with Sodom, Gomorrah, and the surrounding cities. Prior to the destruction of these places, Abraham had a conversation with God. God then revealed to Abraham the possible judgment upon Sodom and Gomorrah, according to what He would find there. Abraham then pleaded with God about the destruction at Sodom for the sake of his nephew Lot, who lived there. Among the words exchanged between God and Abraham, God said to Abraham that He would not destroy Sodom if there were as few as ten righteous people there (Genesis 18:32). So ten righteous people would have saved the entire city from being completely destroyed by the angels of God.

But, before the conversation ended with Abraham pleading for the righteous to be saved, using the amount of ten righteous people, Abraham initially began pleading with God using the amount of fifty righteous people (Genesis 18:24). In the following verse we can see that the search for righteous people was first to be made according to God's words, "If I find." In Genesis, chapter 18, verse 26, God's answer to Abraham was,

> "If I find in Sodom fifty righteous within the city, then
> I will spare all the place for their sakes."

Being that God stated the words, "If I find...fifty righteous," it means that He went *looking* in the city, *to find them.* God went into Sodom to search (probe, examine) their hearts and minds. Only one man was found to be righteous, which was Abraham's nephew, Lot. Only he and his family made it out of the city alive, escaping God's judgment of death and destruction.

Likewise, as God searched hearts and minds before the judgment of the flood, and of Sodom and Gomorrah, He will also be searching hearts before, and probably during, the wrath and judgments of the tribulation. It's one thing He does in His righteousness.

God Searched David's Heart

When Saul, the first anointed king of Israel, kept disobeying God, God searched for someone else to be shepherd and king over His people. The Spirit of God searched out another heart. I'll share some amazing facts that I have learned about this search. In 1 Samuel, chapter 13, verses 13–14, we read these words of Samuel the prophet to King Saul,

> "And Samuel said to Saul, Thou hast done foolishly:
> thou hast not kept the commandment of the LORD

thy God, which he commanded thee: for now would the LORD have established thy kingdom upon Israel for ever."

"But now thy kingdom shall not continue: the LORD hath sought him a man after his own heart, and the LORD hath commanded him to be captain over his people."

Samuel revealed to Saul what God had done. He told him, "the LORD hath sought him a man after his own heart." The Spirit of the living God went and "sought him a man." Personally, I believe this to be an amazing thought to understand. What does it mean for God to seek a man? What is it like for God to go looking for someone? Consider what is involved in seeking out anything. If we were to seek (look for) something in life, what would we do?

A woman, for example, who seeks out clothing will travel to local clothing stores and began looking. This is actually one definition of search: to travel around and look. We look at shirts, skirts, pants, sweaters, dresses, and whatever else we desire. We observe the materials that the clothes are made from, the colors, the shapes, and prices. We search for what satisfies our heart's desire. Correct? Usually, many things are considered in the search. Consider also that we do not purchase and take home all clothing in the stores, but only the items which fulfill what our heart desires. Many of us would like to take home almost all of the clothing within the stores, but truthfully, not all of it satisfies each of our desires.

Perhaps a better example would be a man who seeks out a new truck. He will travel to truck lots and began his search. The colors, sizes, makes, models, details about the motor, and prices will be looked at and considered. Also, the interior with its details will be looked at and considered, just as the Holy Spirit looks inside at the heart of a person (probing) to see what's there. Not all trucks will be purchased, but only one, probably. A man makes the decision according to what satisfies his heart's desire. Correct?

When we understand better what searching involves, we can then better understand what was involved when the Spirit of God went among men in the land and "sought him a man." As previously mentioned, to search, or seek, also means to travel around and investigate. This is what God did when He sought someone to be king of His people, and His heart's desire was satisfied when He found the heart of David, "a man after his own heart." God found a man who was looking for Him.

How did God know that David was after His heart? This is a good question. Think about the areas God searches, which are the thoughts and heart. When God searched David's thoughts, He found they were directed toward Him. David thought about God, often. This indicated he was after God. That pleased God. Consider what the psalmist wrote in Psalm, chapter 10, verse 4: "The wicked, through the pride of his countenance, will not seek after God: God is not in all his thoughts." Notice it says that God is not in "all his thoughts." In the minds of the born again believers are continuous thoughts of God.

This is a main difference between the mind of a saved person, and the mind of those who are not saved and sealed by the Holy Spirit. The redeemed will think about God before, during, and after cooking. The redeemed will think about God before, during, and after work. The redeemed think about God before, during, and after driving, and so forth. The redeemed think of God throughout their day, and this is on a daily basis. He becomes the center of all our thoughts. In Malachi, chapter 3, verse 6, God said,

"For I am the LORD, I change not."

God has always been searching hearts, and He still searches them today. I now sometimes wonder when God had last searched my thoughts, or when He might search again. Consider what Jesus said in Luke, chapter 19, verse 10,

"For the Son of man is come to seek and to save that which was lost."

Jesus came *seeking,* and saving. The Holy Spirit remains the same. Let's take another close look at some details about God looking into people's hearts. When Samuel the prophet initially anointed David to be king of Israel, something took place that reveals more to us about when God searches hearts. In this we can see not only something about the men of the Bible, but also the God of the Bible.

In 1 Samuel, chapter 16, verse 1, God told Samuel to fill his horn with oil and go to "Jesse the Bethlehemite," David's father. Samuel would then anoint the one whom God had chosen to be the next king of Israel, in the family's presence. Initially, God had not given a name to Samuel, therefore Samuel did not know which of his sons were chosen. God was going to reveal the chosen one at the time he was in his presence. In 1 Samuel, chapter 16, verses 4–7, we read,

> "And Samuel did that which the LORD spake, and came to Beth'-le-hem. And the elders of the town trembled at his coming, and said, Comest thou [you come] peaceably?"

> "And he said, Peaceably: I am come to sacrifice unto the LORD: sanctify yourselves, and come with me to the sacrifice. And he sanctified Jesse and his sons, and called them to the sacrifice."

> "And it came to pass, when they were come, that he looked on E-li'-ab, and said, Surely the LORD's anointed is before him [Jehovah]."

> "But the LORD said unto Samuel, Look not on his countenance, or on the height of his stature; because I have refused him: for the LORD seeth [sees] not as man seeth; for man looketh [looks] on the outward appearance, but the LORD looketh on the heart."

When Jesse and his sons arrived at the sacrifice, we read that Samuel "looked on E-li'-ab," David's brother. From what he observed in appearance it prompted him to think and say, "Surely the Lord's anointed is before him [the LORD]." Samuel looked at the outward appearance of E-li'-ab and assumed he was the one. The man's appearance must have been more kingly. But, either hearing Samuel's words, or knowing his thoughts (he may have said this out aloud in front of E-li'-ab), God immediately corrected Samuel in telling him,

> "Look not on his countenance, or on the height of his stature; because I have refused him."

Here's where we get a good glimpse of someone being refused by God. God told Samuel, "I have refused him." Notice the past tense, "refused." By the time Samuel saw E-li'-ab arrive on the scene he was already refused, and David chosen. God had refused a man for service. What this reveals is that when God searched the hearts in the land and came to E-li'-ab, He kept searching, because E-li'-ab was refused. The question to ask at this point is why did God refuse the son of Jesse who apparently looked kingly to Samuel? What was the deciding factor of acceptance and refusal? Reading the second half of verse 7, it tells us,

> "for the Lord seeth [sees] not as man seeth; for man looketh on the outward appearance, but the Lord looketh on the heart."

Samuel did what we do. We surely look at the physical appearance and assume things quite often, unless we have matured enough in the Lord not to do so. As we look on the outside of a person, God is looking on the inside. God is not interested in the sun glasses, the earrings, the boots, the curls or dye in the hair, or even the parting of the hair. He goes beyond the appearance and looks inside. "The Lord looketh on the heart," which tells us that the deciding factor was what He found in the heart, or what wasn't found.

This helps explain the statement of Jesus, in John, chapter 6, verse 44, in which He said, "No man can come to me, except the Father which hath sent me draw him." The only way in which a person can come to Jesus is if God draws the person to Him. God looks into the hearts, and when He finds a willing heart, He'll begin to draw. People may not realize when God is drawing, but if a person comes to Christ and accepts Him, God has drawn. I have both seen, and heard of, God trying to draw some people, but they rejected.

God wanted a man after His own heart, and apparently in His search God found that E-li'-ab wasn't after His heart. Jesse then brought each of his sons in front of Samuel for the choosing. 1 Samuel, chapter 16, verses 8-10 tell us,

> "Then Jesse called A-bin'-a-dab, and made him pass before Samuel. And he said, Neither hath [has] the LORD chosen this."

> "Then Jesse made Sham'-mah to pass by. And he said, Neither hath the LORD chosen this."

> "Again, Jesse made seven of his sons to pass before Samuel. And Samuel said unto Jesse, The LORD hath not chosen these."

David was not present at the time his other brothers were brought before Samuel. As the seven brothers were passed in front of Samuel, it seems there was no prompting nor words that came to him from God, which indicated they were not chosen. But, when David was sent for and brought in front of Samuel (v. 12), the words of the Lord came to him:

> "The LORD said, Arise, anoint him: for this is he."

When the chosen one showed up, it's written that God's voice came forth. Among all the hearts that were searched, there was something in David that pleased God, which was his interest in God. What was found in the heart determined God's choosing. Enlightening, isn't it?

God Searched Hezekiah's Heart

Hezekiah was another man written of having had his heart searched by God. In 2 Chronicles, chapter 32, verses 30–31, it reveals one way in which God searches what is in our hearts. It is important for us to know that God will do this.

> "This same Hezekiah also stopped the upper watercourse of Gi'-hon, and brought it straight down to the west side of the city of David. And Hezekiah prospered in all his works."

> "Howbeit in the business of the ambassadors of the princes of Babylon, who sent unto him to enquire of the wonder that was done in the land, God left him, to try him, that he might know all that was in his heart."

God was interested in finding out "all that was in his heart," and notice how He did this. In verse 31 it says, "God left him, to try him." For Him to leave Hezekiah, it means He was there with him, yet pulled away for the testing. God tested him when he was "in the business of the ambassadors of the princes of Babylon," by temporarily withdrawing His presence from him. When God's presence was withdrawn from the man, whatever was in his heart would then show forth and be known.

Therefore, when God is in the process of finding out what is in our hearts, He may remove His presence from us to do so. Consider that when the Holy Spirit is upon a child of God, God's characteristics—wisdom, joy, kindness, selflessness, faith, and so forth—will then manifest. But when the Holy Spirit is not manifesting what may show up is anger, pride, lust, selfishness, and other sinful traits.

I'll share something the Holy Spirit revealed to me. This is wisdom, which means insight. We can learn to evaluate, or judge, ourselves well by discerning when we are not in the Spirit, and paying close attention to what behavior surfaces at that time. When the Spirit is manifesting, pay careful attention to how you are changed in His presence. Try to notice the wisdom, the faith, the patience, the knowledge, the intense love, the willingness to forgive, the thankfulness, the boldness, or the kindness that shows up along with His presence. All these fruits (and more) are in abundance in His presence. When His Spirit rests upon us, we feel holiness, because we are in His presence. When He is not manifesting we may experience the opposite of what He brings. When He is not manifesting, what traits do you experience? Evaluate yourself.

For example, when the Spirit is fully resting upon me I become very bold and and perhaps a little loud, faith escalates tremendously, insight of the spiritual realm dramatically increases, I love everyone greatly, wisdom seems to flow from me, I have an eagerness to forgive everyone thoroughly, and I want to give and bless people.

But when I don't feel the manifestation of His presence, I do not want to give as eagerly (greed in the heart), a couple of people I don't feel like loving too much (lack of love in the heart), and boldness and faith seem to diminish a bit (doubt and fear present in the heart). When the Holy Spirit is not manifesting and characteristics opposite the fruits of the Spirit begin to show up, those are issues in the heart that God wants us to work on cleansing.

God Searched Hearts When Prayer Was Made

Here is another enlightening fact concerning when God searches the hearts. There is evidence in Jeremiah's writings that God will probably search the heart prior to giving an answer to prayer. In Jeremiah, chapter 42, we read of a remnant of Judah (Jeremiah 42:15) that lived near Bethlehem after Babylon conquered the land. The remnant approached Jeremiah the prophet to ask God for direction in their lives at that time, because of the circumstances in the land. They were considering heading out to Egypt, yet they approached Jeremiah first to go to God for them in prayer.

Again, we will see where God took time to search hearts. If you aren't looking for this in these verses, it's likely you'll miss the clues that are given. As we read of God searching hearts before giving an answer to their prayer request, it helps us to know that God will want to know what's in our hearts when we pray and ask Him for things. This may bring enlightenment to verse 3 in James, chapter 4, concerning asking for something "amiss." In Jeremiah, chapter 42, verses 1–3, it reads,

"Then all the captains of the forces, and Jo-ha'-nan the son of Ka-re'-ah, and Jez-a-ni'-ah the son of Ho- sha'-iah, and all the people from the least even unto the greatest, came near,"

"And said unto Jeremiah the prophet, Let, we beseech thee, our supplication be accepted before thee [you], and pray for us unto the LORD thy [your] God, even for all this remnant; (for we are left but a few of many, as thine eyes do behold us:)"

"That the LORD thy God may shew [show] us the way wherein we may walk, and the thing that we may do."

Those who still remained in the land made a decision to ask Jeremiah for counsel from God about their future at that point in their lives. They didn't know God themselves to go to Him in prayer. It seemed good that they desired counsel from God, as if they were ready to begin turning to Him at that time. But were they sincere in their request? What was in their minds when they asked for prayer to God? Scripture reveals that we cannot hide what's in our hearts from God. Verses 4–6 then say,

"Then Jeremiah the prophet said unto them, I have heard you; behold, I will pray unto the LORD your God according to your words; and it shall come to pass, that whatsoever thing the LORD shall answer you, I will declare it unto you; I will keep nothing back from you."

"Then they said to Jeremiah, The LORD be a true and faithful witness between us, if we do not even according to all things for the which the LORD thy God shall send thee to us."

"Whether it be good, or whether it be evil, we will obey the voice of the Lord our God, to whom we send thee; that it may be well with us, when we obey the voice of the LORD our God."

I want to point out a few things at this point. In verses 2-3, when the people asked Jeremiah to pray to his God for them they said to Jeremiah, "thy God." They thought of Him as being Jeremiah's God, not their own. In verse 4, Jeremiah spoke of Him as being their God. In verse 5, the remnant still referred to Him as Jeremiah's God. In verse 6, it shows that the remnant began to say "our God," whether they meant it or not. They had drifted so far from God, they did not know Him anymore. Verse 7 goes on to say,

> "And it came to pass after ten days, that the word of the LORD came unto Jeremiah."

> "Then called he Jo-ha'-nan the son of Ka-re'-ah, and all the captains of the forces which were with him, and all the people from the least even to the greatest."

I want to draw attention to the number of days that passed before Jeremiah received an answer from God. Scripture reveals there were times when God's answers came quickly, after three weeks, or even immediately. In this case it was "after ten days, that the word of the LORD came," and they received their answer. Why the ten day wait? The Holy Spirit drew my attention to the ten days. The longer my attention was held on the thought of ten days, the more I realized there was a significance to the amount of days. There is a reason why God did not answer the prayer request for ten days.

After the ten days, Jeremiah heard from God. He then told the people that if they stayed in the land God would build them up. He also said they should not be afraid of the king of Babylon, because He would give them favor, save them, and deliver them. God also warned them not to go to Egypt, where they were initially thinking of going. God warned them that they would die if they went there (42:16).

This leads us to verse 20, in which Jeremiah was still relaying God's message to them. This verse contains a clue as to why the ten day wait on God's answer. Notice the mention of "hearts" in the next verse. In chapter 42, verse 20, we are given that Jeremiah told them this,

> "For ye dissembled in your hearts, when ye sent me unto the LORD your God."

Notice what Jeremiah realized about those who asked him to pray for them. He said to them, "For ye dissembled in your hearts, when ye sent me." To dissemble means to have false intentions, which means they were not serious in their "hearts" about their claim to follow God's counsel. But at what point did they have false intentions? Jeremiah said to them, "when ye sent me unto the LORD." When they initially requested that he pray to God for them, they did not have full intentions in their hearts to obey what they would be told to do.

They did not want God in their lives up to that point, and that's where we can see there was a purpose in the ten day wait. The Lord did not answer for ten days, because the Spirit of God went among the remnant and searched what was in their hearts. What He had found was fear in their hearts (Jeremiah 42:11), and they were contemplating going to Egypt (Jeremiah 42:13, 14). He found dissembling (false intentions) in their hearts.

"After ten days, that the word of the LORD came unto Jeremiah." For ten days God searched the thoughts and intents of their hearts, therefore, the Lord's answer was according to His findings. In Hebrews, chapter 4, verse 12, it says this about the intentions of the heart:

> "For the word of God…is a discerner of the thoughts and intents of the heart."

The word "discerner" in this verse is from the Greek word *kritikos*, meaning decisive. This is where we get our English words *critical, critic,* and *criterion* from. It refers to being fit for judging. The Word of God, which is the living Word, determines and judges our thoughts and intentions. Scripture also states that Jesus searches our thoughts and intentions, and He was born and came forth as the Living Word. He looks into our hearts and minds, discerns the intents, and judges according to what He finds. This He did with the people before the flood of Noah's days, in Sodom and Gomorrah, David's family, and Hezekiah.

I have come to realize that when God finds sin in me, the sin becomes very evident to me; it begins to clearly come to mind, repeatedly. The Holy Spirit is then revealing what He has found, and I know it's time to repent. He is the One who leads us to repent (Romans 2:4). It's good to know this, and to know what He is doing.

God Tested the Wandering Hearts

Deuteronomy, chapter 8, verses 1 and 2 also offer enlightenment about God searching hearts. As the Israelites wandered around in the wilderness, it was not in vain. God was working on the hearts that He was so interested in. In these verses are words spoken to the Israelites before they went into the Promised Land. It states,

> "All the commandments which I command thee this day shall ye observe to do, that ye [you] may live, and multiply, and go in and possess the land which the LORD sware unto your fathers."

> "And thou shalt [you shall] remember all the way which the LORD thy God led thee these forty years in the wilderness, to humble thee [you], and to prove thee, to know what was in thine [your] heart, whether thou wouldest [would] keep his commandments, or no."

In verse 2, it reveals why God led the Israelites through the wilderness for forty years. They were told it was "to prove thee, to know what was in thine heart." What we read here is like the case with Hezekiah, when God tested him to see what manifested in his heart. Well, God also proved, or tested, the Israelites to see what was in their hearts. Do you see how interested God is in our hearts? The more we pull out of the Bible, the clearer this subject becomes.

The generation of Israelites who walked out of Egypt kept failing God's tests. They murmured and complained continuously. They lacked belief in God's words, turned against the anointed leaders, and God. For forty years God heard what came out of their mouths from their hearts. It was very displeasing to Him. In Hebrews chapter 3 it says that God was grieved with that generation. God decided they weren't allowed to enter the Promised Land. However, the next generation was able to enter. Verse 2 reveals that humbling them was also part of the process, and to know "whether thou wouldest keep his commandments, or no."

A very enlightening fact to know is that God is going to spend the time it takes to know who will keep his Commandments. Just as God tested them to see if they would keep His commandments, He may prove us to see if we will continue in His teachings.

God Will Search Your Heart

Do you know how interested God is in the thought of your heart? Very much so. You are as important to Him as were Hezekiah, the Israelites, King David, and the others. It is very likely that God has visited you lately to see what is in your heart and thoughts. If He hasn't, you can know that He is coming to search what is in there. This is the mysterious search that He has been on for thousands of years, and He's not finished yet. Referring back to Jesus' words in Revelation, chapter 2, verse 23, He said,

"I am he which searcheth the reins [minds] and hearts."

He's coming to search us, there's no doubt. He may have searched your heart yesterday, or last week. What is in our hearts will shape who we are, and it matters greatly to Him. There are plenty of verses in the Bible that help explain that we are shaped by what's in our hearts. Proverbs, chapter 23, verses 6–7 tell us,

"Eat thou not the bread of him that hath [has] an evil eye, neither desire thou his dainty meats:"

> "For as he thinketh [thinks] in his heart, so is he: Eat and drink, saith [says] he to thee; but his heart is not with thee [you]."

An evil eye is mentioned both here and by Jesus, in Mark, chapter 7, verses 21–22. The writer of this verse and Jesus both say that having an evil eye is a result of having evil in the heart. Here in Proverbs, it refers to immorality, according to the definitions of the Hebrew word that is used. The writer understood that the evil was in the heart and was divinely inspired to write,

> "For as he thinketh in his heart, so is he."

As we think in our hearts, so are we. Before I accepted Jesus Christ as Lord and Savior, I used to have the sin of bitterness in my heart. I had bitter thoughts that kept surfacing, and it was actually controlling my life. My actions were bitter, which resulted from the thoughts of bitterness that I had. The Lord has led me out of that sin. It took about a year and a half or so for God to help me recognize it, teach me many details about it, and get it out. It is no longer in my thoughts to be bitter, therefore, it is no longer in my heart, and no longer part of my character anymore. Hallelujah!

If we think fearful thoughts, we will be fearful. If we think prideful thoughts, we will be prideful. If we think lustful thoughts, we will be lustful. If we think greedy thoughts, we will be greedy. As we think in our hearts, so will we be, and Jesus spends time with us to help us renew our thoughts. This is mentioned in Romans, chapter 12, verse 2:

> "And be not conformed to this world: but be ye transformed by the renewing of your mind, that ye may prove what is that good, and acceptable, and perfect, will of God."

When you move into the family of God, you are to change by "the renewing of your mind." When thoughts change, the person will change, good or bad. The mind is the area that Jesus searches, and is an area the Devil will attack. When we clean out our thoughts, we are cleaning out our hearts, and peace in the mind follows. King David apparently knew of this mystery concerning God's interest in knowing what was in the hearts of men, because he wrote this in Psalm, chapter 139, verses 23 and 24,

> "Search me, O God, and know my heart: try me, and know my thoughts:"

> "And see if there be any wicked way in me, and lead me in the way everlasting."

David invited God to come search his heart. He knew God investigated everyone's heart, and of the importance to God of a spiritual (thought and heart) cleaning. When God finds sin in His children, He brings it to their attention for the purpose of leading them out of the sin. Romans, chapter 2, verse 4 tells us,

> "Or despisest thou [do you despise] the riches of his goodness and forbearance and longsuffering; not knowing that the goodness of God leadeth thee [leads you] to repentance?"

Repentance is turning away from sin, which is a requirement of God. When we accept Jesus into our hearts and become sealed by the Holy Spirit, we are surrendering our life to Him. He then begins to push the evil out and work holiness in. It is God's goodness that "leadeth thee to repentance." The moment at which we begin to recognize a sin that we are committing and are desiring to turn from the sin, it's God that has led us there. Without the Holy Spirit we don't know what we're doing wrong, or why we have the problems we may be having, but God has the answers for us. He has all the answers. He will lead us to repentance of what will harm us now, and what He will judge against on the day of judgment. Matthew, chapter 15, verse 18, tells us,

> "But those things which proceed out of the mouth come forth from the heart."

According to Jesus, whatever we speak reveals what's in our hearts. We should probably do as David did: ask God often to search us and lead us to repent.

If you haven't done so and would like to surrender your heart to Jesus, become saved for eternity, and begin a spiritual cleansing, don't delay doing so. God sent Jesus to die on the cross to take the punishment for our sins. All we have to do is accept this truth, confess it, and accept the gift of His Holy Spirit, which He gives to anyone who asks for it. Just confess that you believe and give your heart and life to God. He's waiting on you.

Prayer for Salvation

God, I believe that You are the One true God, and I believe
that Jesus was Your Son who died on the cross
for the punishment of my sins. I confess that I have sinned
against You and need forgiveness. Will You forgive me
for my sins, come into my heart, and save me? I surrender
my life to You today. God, will You baptize me
with Your Holy Spirit, teach me about You, and show
me how to follow You? Today, I confess Jesus as
my Lord and my Savior. In Jesus' name I pray, amen.

Prayer for God to Search You
(Psalm 139:23–24)

Search me, O God, and know my heart: try me, and know my
thoughts: And see if there be any wicked way in me,
and lead me in the way everlasting. In Jesus' name I pray, amen.

Chapter 3

Heaven Is Like Hidden Treasure

What comes to mind when you think of hidden treasure? What comes to mind when you think of heaven? Well, Jesus put these two together in a parable He spoke to compare someone finding the kingdom of heaven, to someone finding hidden treasure in a field. This parable is only one verse, yet it completely sums up what takes place when a person truly comes in contact with Jesus, the King of Kings, and the kingdom of heaven.

As I was reading this verse while preparing a Sunday School lesson, the Holy Spirit held my attention on this verse for quite some time and gave me much deeper insight into this parable. There is much to consider in this illustration. So let's dig into Scripture to find some knowledge about the hidden treasures of heaven, and see what Jesus gave us in this verse.

Heaven Is Hidden

This verse will be studied in sections to consider the given knowledge in it about heaven being hidden, when it is found, and the effects on the one who finds it. Other scriptures will also be given throughout this chapter to help bring clarity on this subject. In Matthew, chapter 13, verse 44, we find this parable of Jesus:

> "Again, the kingdom of heaven is like unto treasure
> hid in a field; the which when a man hath [has] found,

he hideth [hides], and for joy thereof goeth [goes] and selleth [sells] all that he hath, and buyeth [buys] that field."

Notice that Jesus said the kingdom of heaven is like "treasure hid." Heaven is such a mystery because—it's hidden. God has it hidden. This is a very good way to help us understand heaven, and also to help explain it. To be hidden means to be concealed, not seen, or not revealed. Many people believe in heaven and God, but have no knowledge of either, because they are concealed, or hidden.

I clearly remember the days in which heaven was a complete mystery to me. When I heard the word heaven throughout my childhood years and into my teens, I knew and believed that there was such a place, but my knowledge stopped there. I understood nothing at all about it. At the age of 29 I found heaven, and its glorious King. Scripture does confirm that heaven is hidden, but it also reveals that it can be found. Some Scriptures say God has to be searched for diligently with the whole heart to be found. For example, in Jeremiah, chapter 29, verse 13, God told the Israelites,

"And ye shall seek me, and find me, when ye shall search for me with all your heart."

In this verse we see that God mentioned finding Him as well as seeking Him. Do you see that God wants to be searched for, and that He wants all of the heart in on the search for Him? Those who seek God will discover that He wants to be upfront and personal in each of their lives. He wants to be in close fellowship with us, and He wants all, not part of us. One way to understand God's desire to be number one in our lives is to understand that He wants a relationship, and He knows what's needed for a successful relationship. He created us to have relationships. God wants all of our heart invested in a relationship with Him.

Consider a husband and his wife in marriage. What if the husband or the wife, or both, were not wholly interested in the relationship? What if either, or both, invested only half their time, half their love, and half their efforts towards each other throughout the marriage? What would become of a relationship such as that? According to the word of God, we reap what we sow (Galatians 6:7), and this includes our relationship with our Creator. We will get out of it only what we put into it. In Matthew, chapter 6, verse 33, Jesus said,

> "But seek ye first the kingdom of God, and his righteousness; and all these things shall be added unto you."

Jesus instructs us to first seek God's kingdom. God wants this to be our priority in life. God desires that we look for Him, and listen for Him daily. When we seek God's kingdom, we discover that righteousness is there, to learn it and walk in it. Prior to this verse we read that water, food, and clothes, which God knows we all need, are to be added to the life of those who first seek righteousness and the kingdom from which it comes. "These things shall be added unto you," Jesus said.

Heaven is like hidden treasure, and if it's searched for, it can be found. Another verse that helps us to know that God is interested in our interest and search for Him is in Psalm, chapter 14, verse 2. In this, King David wrote,

> "The Lord looked down from heaven upon the children of men, to see if there were any that did understand, and seek God."

David, who knew the King of heaven, revealed that He looks down at us on earth. One reason He does so is to see who is looking for Him. He created us and is interested in us, but who is interested in Him? That He wants to know. Have you looked for God in your life? Do you seek Him out these days? God looks to see if you do, and He knows if you're not. If you choose to search for heaven, you can find it. Heaven's King will know if you are looking.

When Heaven Is Found

The focus will now be on when a man has found the treasure, and its comparison to what takes place when someone actually finds heaven, and its King. In Matthew, chapter 13, verse 44, again the parable states,

> "Again, the kingdom of heaven is like unto treasure hid in a field; the which when a man hath [has] found, he hideth, and for joy thereof goeth [goes] and selleth [sells] all that he hath [has], and buyeth [buys] that field."

Let's look at the phrase, "which when a man hath found." Though the kingdom of heaven is a hidden mystery, it can indeed be found, and is found by many. This encounter with heaven and its King has an amazing, transforming effect on the individual who has truly found it, and its treasures. As we read in this parable, it is notable that Jesus made a point to mention that after the person has found the treasure (heaven), "he hideth" it. Why? The treasure is found in a field that does not belong to him, therefore, the treasure is not rightfully his, yet. He hides it, and notice in the example what the Lord says he does:

> "for joy thereof goeth and selleth [goes and sells] all that he hath [has], and buyeth that field."

He is moved by such great joy at what he has found that he "selleth all that he hath," to get the field with its treasure into his possession. That's a great amount of joy, which comes from the touch of the Holy Spirit. It's written in Acts, chapter 2, verse 45, that believers sold their possessions and gave to those in need, after hearing the gospel and believing (Acts 2: 45). But consider what is written here in Romans, chapter 14, verse 17, which says,

> "For the kingdom of God is not meat [food] and drink; but righteousness, and peace, and joy in the Holy Ghost."

The kingdom of heaven, which is the treasure in the parable, is "joy in the Holy Ghost." God gives His Holy Spirit to those who accept Jesus as His Son, and the infilling of the Holy Spirit brings amazing joy to the hearts of those who receive Him. The joy that the man in the example encountered moved him to do something dramatic. He had come across something in life that he deemed to be so much more worthy than all he'd had in his life up to that point. An encounter with heaven does this to the heart of a person that truly finds heaven.

Can you see the spiritual side of this example? With God's amazing joy resting in his heart, he gets rid of what he has to so that he could get hold of and keep what he has found. In this we can see that a true encounter with God will lead us to set our hearts and minds on Him, not the the things of the world. This parable reveals this.

This is what it's like when a person finds God, and the kingdom of heaven. The things of God are hidden, but if we seek God, He says we will find Him. There are many people that have never heard a message such as this about heaven. There are many people who need to know that if they want to find heaven and God, they can, here and now.

Once we receive the Holy Spirit from God, we gain deliverance, freedom, and a relationship with the Christ that becomes more valuable than anything else. The reason is because Jesus makes such a powerful impact within the person who comes in contact with Him, that nothing else can compare with that experience. Nothing!

The things in this world become less desirable than what Jesus, the King of heaven, has to offer. That's when our grip on this world loosens, and the grip on the treasures of heaven tighten. This parable reveals the amazing change that takes place in the life of the one who truly encounters the King of glory. There are those who may appear to have found heaven and its King, but the actions in their life do not add up to reflect the actions of the one given in this parable.

The Holy Spirit had repeatedly led my attention to the part of this parable that reveals where the treasure was found, which was in a field that did not belong to the one who found it. Consider the fact that Jesus didn't give an example with the treasure being found on the property of him who found it. That would have made it rightfully his to begin with, and too easy to claim it. Correct?

I have found that in times past, before the banking system we have today, it was common for the wealthy to bury their wealth in places such as beneath their homes or in fields to hide it for certain purposes. If he who buried it died in battle, or due to some other cause, the whereabouts of the treasure would likely remain unknown, and very likely be in a field. This parable may be referring to such a treasure.

The treasure represents heaven, and God owns heaven; therefore, God is the owner of the field in the parable. Jesus clearly revealed that the treasure could not be taken immediately; he had to let go of "all that he hath" to gain it. To have the treasure (heaven) become his, it cost him everything he had, which was his joyous decision.

He who finds this treasure in life will have to make a decision to let go of the things of this world and hold on to the treasure of heaven, or let the treasure go. Can you see this truth? There are other verses that support this message. Consider that if the man hadn't sold everything to go purchase that property with the treasure, it would *never* have become his. That's the way in which Jesus stated the parable. In Matthew, chapter 6, verses 19–21, Jesus told us,

> "Lay not up for yourselves treasures upon earth, where moth and rust doth [does] corrupt, and where thieves break through and steal:"

> "But lay up for yourselves treasures in heaven, where neither moth nor rust doth [does] corrupt, and where thieves do not break through nor steal:"

> "For where your treasure is, there will your heart be also."

Jesus enlightens us to the fact that our hearts will be exactly where our treasure is. So, if you set up treasures in heaven, your heart will be there. If you set up for yourself earthly treasures, your heart will be there. If we can discern what our heart (thoughts) is set on, it can help determine what we are treasuring, and God wants our hearts to be set on Him. Truly, there are no exceptions. None!

It is not difficult to quickly learn to store up things in life, especially in this generation. Here in America there is so much offered to society that can lead us to want to store up stuff, both great and small possessions. But how are we to store a treasure in heaven, a place where we have not been yet? There are details within the remaining verses to be looked at in this chapter that will help guide us in understanding heaven's treasure a little better, and to know how to store something there. In 1 John, chapter 2, verse 15, we read,

> "Love not the world, neither the things that are in the world. If any man love the world, the love of the Father is not in him."

This is a clear message. We either love God, or the world. Our hearts cannot be swaying between the two. He doesn't accept that. If we are going to learn to love God, we will have to learn to let go of worldly things, as seen in the parable of the hidden treasure. This verse clearly informs us that if we love worldly things, our love is not with God. Satan is written of as being the god of this world, and we need to let go of all that God leads us to let go of. This is because Jesus is to set up His kingdom on earth at a soon appointed time, and that is what the children of God are to inherit and focus on.

Being Rich with God

In Scripture there is a parable of a rich man whose soul was required of him, and he had many goods in his life that did not make him rich with God. These verses offer much more to consider about what God says our focus in life should be on. There is a very clear message in this parable about treasures on earth, and treasure in heaven. Luke, chapter 12, verses 13–21, is where we find this parable. Beginning with verses 13–14, it says,

> "And one of the company said unto him [Jesus], Master, speak to my brother, that he divide the inheritance with me."

"And he said unto him, Man, who made me a judge or
a divider over you?"

Luke wrote of someone concerned about a family inheritance.
We see here that Jesus wasn't at all concerned about the man's earthly
inheritance, but rather warned of the dangers of covetousness, in the
next verse. Jesus addressed the concerned man's request with these
words in verse 15,

"And he said unto them, Take heed, and beware of
covetousness: for a man's life consisteth not in the
abundance of the things which he possesseth [possesses]."

Jesus responded with "beware of covetousness," and addressed the
issue of thinking highly about having an abundance of possessions in
life. God's not interested in our stuff; He's interested in us. It will do us
good to know that every day when we wake up, God is focused on us,
not our stuff. Jesus gave an example of being rich in two ways: earthly
riches, and heavenly riches. He then proceeded to give a parable to
help them understand what God deems to be important in life. What
He gave in this parable revealed what riches need to be gained before
facing life after death. In this we can know the mind of God. In verses
16–18, He said,

"And he spake [spoke] a parable unto them, saying, The
ground of a certain rich man brought forth plentifully:"

"And he thought within himself, saying, What shall
I do, because I have no room where to bestow [store]
my fruits?"

"And he said, This will I do: I will pull down my barns,
and build greater; and there will I bestow all my fruits
and my goods."

In this example the man had such an abundance of provision that
he "thought within himself" about having the room to store it all. So,

what's wrong with this? The thought of his heart was directed on his goods and himself. His focus was on how much he had, and how he was going to pack it away to make sure he was taken care of for future years. Doesn't this sound typical? Then we read in verse 19 where his thoughts were going:

> "And I will say to my soul, Soul, thou hast much goods
> laid up for many years; take thine ease, eat, drink, and
> be merry."

He was ready to sit back and enjoy life "for many years" with all his fruits and goods. He was prepared for the future, on earth. Jesus then brings our attention to this very important thought in verse 20,

> "But God said unto him, Thou [you] fool, this night thy
> [your] soul shall be required of thee: then whose shall
> those things be, which thou hast provided?"

Here the unexpected was to happened. His life on earth was to end when it was "required" of him. His thoughts were to set himself up with provision "for many years" to come. What Jesus revealed was that he was laying up for himself "treasures upon earth," focusing on and trusting in them. But, in this example, Jesus says of God, to the man who had done this, "thou fool." Can you imagine that? What he had done was foolish in the eyes of God, said Jesus. Jesus then ended this example with these words in verse 21, which is a message to us all:

> "So is he that layeth [lays] up treasure for himself, and
> is not rich toward God."

This is God's wisdom for us. This example shows the plans in life of many who are only considering and planning for life on earth, and not beyond. Jesus clearly reveals that a person needs to prepare for something beyond this life. Judgment and accountability await humanity beyond this life. Both God and His will for us needs to be sought and known before we face eternity. We need to learn to be rich with God before we die, so that we are not labeled "thou fool," as the man in the example had been. Jesus specifically stated, "God said unto him, Thou fool." Jesus gave us God's words toward those who do this. He made it a point not to leave this out.

This man was rich in worldly wealth, but he was not "rich toward God" when his life ended. Let's not be fools, but learn to be wise in God's eyes. We should not let stuff steal our hearts from God, but set our hearts on Him; that's real wealth in God's eyes.

This may be difficult for many to consider and accept, but consider and try to name anyone who has taken their business, bank account, or household items with them when they passed on. Did not only their soul leave? Stuff gathered on the earth remains on the earth. James knew and revealed something about being rich with God, in chapter 2, verse 5, saying,

> "Hearken my beloved brethren, Hath [has] not God chosen the poor of this world rich in faith, and heirs of the kingdom which he hath promised to them that love him."

Notice that God has chosen "the poor of this world," yet "rich in faith." There it is. Having faith in God is heavenly wealth. Do you have some of this wealth? We can obtain it while we are here, and yes, we can take it with us, amen! They "that love him" are promised an inheritance in the kingdom, according to this verse. When we search the Scriptures we will find what are riches with God, which are not what we grow up in this world believing to be riches. We are to be seeking Him and His kingdom first. He says He'll provide all of what we need if we do this.

So, are we willing to have faith that God will do what He says? Are we ready to store some treasure in heaven? To gain all we can gain for ourselves means we are putting our hearts and trust into the riches on earth and ourselves, not God. This He doesn't accept. Remember that Jesus said, "For where your treasure is, there will your heart be also" (Matthew 6:21).

Beware of Great Possessions

We will now look into the case of a rich young man with great possessions. This is not a parable, but an illustration that involved a real man with a real hold on his possessions in life. We can compare this actual event with the parable just read. This is a great example. Luke wrote of him as a ruler (Luke 18:18), and Matthew wrote of him as being a young man (Matthew 19:20). Both Matthew and Mark wrote that he had great possessions. Jesus referred to him as having riches (Matthew 10:23–25). In Mark, chapter 10, verses 17–22, there is given a very good example of the serious difficulties of letting go of worldly possessions, and holding on to God instead. It is a very good illustration to read, meditate on, and see through the eyes of God.

In these verses we read of a wealthy young man who got on his knees in the presence of Jesus and asked Him what he needed to do to inherit eternal life (treasures in heaven). In verse 19, Jesus listed the Commandments for him to follow. The rich young man told Jesus he'd kept them since he was young. Then we read this in verses 21–22,

> "Then Jesus beholding him loved him, and said unto him, One thing thou lackest: go thy way, sell whatsoever thou hast [you have], and give to the poor, and thou shalt [you shall] have treasure in heaven: and come, take up the cross, and follow me."

> "And he was sad at that saying, and went away grieved: for he had great possessions."

This man had an interest in the inheritance from God and asked Jesus how to get it. The young man apparently saw to it to follow the Commandments beginning in his youth. But, after hearing the young man's statement, Jesus added a request, in which verse 21 states:

> "sell whatsoever thou hast, and give to the poor, and thou shalt have treasure in heaven."

Notice Jesus told him that "treasure in heaven" would be his by selling all he had, giving to the poor, and following Him. If you recall, this is exactly what the man in the parable of the hidden treasure did. Jesus said this was one thing that he lacked. Was it not enough that he kept all the Commandments?

What was questionable was, could he let go of all his worldly goods and set his heart on "treasure in heaven?" Did the young man think the "treasure in heaven" to be less worthy to hold on to than his earthly ones? This option would not be so difficult for those who don't have much in life to hold on to, but this can be a very difficult decision for those who have much earthly wealth.

But, are we not to have anything in life? Does Jesus want His followers to get rid of everything and become the poor? Is that the message? Consider this thought. Jesus had initially told the rich man to keep the Commandments to inherit eternal life. That was His answer. The young man proclaimed he kept them since he was young. Jesus then requested something that would test his willingness to follow Him. Jesus addressed his stuff. Why?

Remember that Jesus told John that He searches the hearts and minds (Revelation 2:23). Jesus told the young man to let go of his stuff, and when he did what was his response? He was saddened, and walked away from Jesus grieved over the thought of departing from his stuff. What did his response reveal to the One who searches hearts? It revealed what his heart was set on, which was his stuff—not God.

Basically, Jesus searched his heart and exposed what was in there. Jesus said that where our treasure is, that is where our heart will be. From this reading we can see what this young man's heart was set on— treasures on earth. Though he kept the Commandments, his heart was not truly ready to go all the way with Jesus. Something was in his heart coming between him and his Creator—his possessions. A few verses down, in verse 24, Jesus then said to His disciples,

> "Children, how hard is it for them that trust in riches
> to enter into the kingdom of God!"

Notice here He points out that it's the "trust in riches" that is the issue, rather than trusting in God in this life. It's where our faith lies. If you will notice, Jesus did not say that the possessions were the issue, but where the man placed his trust was definitely a major issue to Jesus. Jesus said, "how hard is it for them that trust in riches to enter." He did not say that being rich makes it difficult to enter heaven, but putting trust in the wealth rather than in God can apparently hinder a soul from entering. Faith is vital.

God apparently does not take lightly our misplace of trust. This is something we need to understand about God. If Jesus took the time to find out what he was trusting in, then we can know that trust (faith) is a necessary ingredient that God is looking for in the heart. God takes this very seriously. The man in the Scriptures would not part from the possessions. And what did Jesus tell him? Sell the stuff, and the inheritance is yours.

So, where do we stand in our faith with God? Do we have stuff that clutters our hearts and takes the place of God? Is there no room for God in our hearts? It truly is a very serious matter to God. God has to come first, and we need to learn how to place Him first. God is probably going to test us to see what our trust is in. So, one way to be rich with God, is being "rich in faith."

Learn to Take Your Journey with Faith

I was led by the Holy Spirit to compare the time the Israelites were led out of Egypt with the parable of the hidden treasure, and note the similarities and differences. The man in the parable with hidden treasure got rid of all he had and went after the treasure in the field, the kingdom of heaven. The Israelites, though, would not mentally let go of what they'd had in Egypt to get their treasure in the Promised Land.

When they walked out of Egypt with Moses, they kept complaining about a lack of satisfying provision on their journey to the Promised Land. The Bible says they longed for what they once had in Egypt, which were things such as fish, cucumbers, onions, melons, and leeks (Numbers 11:5). Their given blessings in the Promised Land were not far into the future, but they had to let go and walk away from the provision in Egypt to go get the future blessings of God. This is when they were to put all their trust in God and be rich in faith, knowing they had a promised destination. However, along the way, they would not let go of what they'd had in Egypt; they kept longing for it.

When life became uncomfortable, they wanted to walk away from God and His promises (the treasure), and go back to their provision in a kingdom of darkness, where sin and slavery abounded. Likewise, we are called by God to be led out of Satan's kingdom of darkness, sin, and bondage, and trust Him until the end of our journey, or until He calls us up.

The Hebrews found their God, the hidden treasure in the field, but they wouldn't put their trust in Him and mentally let go of all they'd had in Egypt. They didn't hold on to God and the promises instead. They did not become "rich in faith" on their journey with God. They also did not enter the Promised Land because of this.

Again, where do we stand in the matter of being rich with God? Are we prepared to let go when God prompts us to let go? Are we ready to trust God in every area of our lives until we get to heaven? When situations get tough, are we going to believe in His promises and stand rich in faith? Scripture says, "But without faith it is impossible to please him" (Hebrews 11:6). He's going to try us.

The heart of the rich young man, who had the great possessions, was not set on God, which interfered with gaining God's inheritance. He did not let go of all he had to get the treasure in heaven. He actually walked away from Jesus, back to his great possessions. Consider that. That's all we know, according to Scripture. He laid up treasures on earth for himself, which his heart would not let go of. Jesus saw that but loved him nonetheless. He already loves us, but we have to choose to love Him. It is amazing to know the living God loves, and wants to be loved back—with all the heart. He seeks devoted hearts for His kingdom. In 1 John, chapter 4, verse 10, it reads,

> "Herein is love, not that we loved God, but that he loved us, and sent his Son to be the propitiation for our sins."

God already loves us, just as Jesus loved the young man who had great possessions, but we need to learn to love Him back. The Holy Spirit helps us do this. Jesus was absolutely not interested in the man's stuff, but the condition of his heart. God longs to be first in each of our lives. This is a beautiful fact to realize.

We learn to let go of the things of this world and hold on to Jesus, when we have recognized the tremendous value of heaven's treasure. The evidence that one has truly found heaven, and accepts it, is when he or she begins to let go, and God becomes the center stage in their life. It means that God is—winning the heart.

If you are not sure what you need to let go of, bring it to God in prayer, ask Him, and have faith that He will teach you. If you ask anything according to His will, He will hear and grant the petitions (1 John 5:14). He wants your heart set on Him.

If you know nothing about God and heaven and would like to find this treasure, you must believe Jesus was the Son of God, that He died on the cross for our sins, and was raised from the dead. If you believe this and confess it aloud from the heart, He will save you (Romans 10:9), and reveal Himself to you. Scripture says that it is God's pleasure to give us the kingdom of heaven (Luke 12:32).

When you make your confession of belief and ask Him for His Holy Spirit, He will then place His Spirit upon you, as He says He will. You will then begin to see what heaven consists of, and you will begin to perceive God around you, who has been there the whole time. Only God can reveal this to you. If you desire to be saved, below is a prayer for you to pray out loud to God for salvation, and guidance in laying up treasure in heaven. The treasures of heaven will then become available to you. Then read the Bible daily. God will make Himself known to you through His Word.

Prayer for Salvation

God, I believe You are the One true God who created heaven and
earth. I believe Jesus was Your Son, who died on the cross for
the punishment of my sins. Will You forgive me for all my sins, come
into my heart, baptize me with Your Holy Spirit, and save me?
Will You lead me and teach me how to become rich with You, show me
Your treasures in heaven, and teach me how to set my heart on
them? Today, I confess Jesus as my Lord and Savior. Thank You
for hearing my prayer. In Jesus' name I pray, amen.

Chapter 4

The Mystery behind "Ears to Hear"

One of the most amazing revelations I have received was about these words of Jesus, "He that hath ears to hear, let him hear," in Luke chapter 14, verse 35, although this saying is in several other places in the New Testament. Revelation, chapter 2, verse 7, offers clarity on what hearing ears will hear. In this verse Jesus said it this way,

> "He that hath an ear, let him hear what the Spirit saith [says]."

According to these words, a person who has an ear to hear will hear "what the Spirit saith." So, when the Holy Spirit speaks, the hearing ear will hear Him. Would you like to know why some people hear the Holy Spirit, and others do not? I'd read over this saying of Jesus for years, but the Holy Spirit had not led me to any other place in the Bible where there was an explanation for those special "ears to hear." I wanted to know what, and whom He was talking about. Why couldn't everyone hear? Why did He address certain ears? Were these specially gifted people? Were the messages only meant for people with good spiritual ears? What did that statement mean?

The answer came when I was preparing a Sunday School lesson on Ezekiel, and sometime later the Lord confirmed the revelation with His words in the New Testament. The Old Testament Jews had the same "hearing" problem as did the people in the New Testament. It is also the same problem with people today. The reason for hearing, or not hearing (spiritually), is the same among all generations as you will see in these given verses. For me, this was an amazing revelation about who has "ears to hear." I pray that you are enlightened through this reading, and better understand what is happening in the hearts and minds of people who hear, and those who don't.

In 1 Corinthians, chapter 13, verse 9, the apostle Paul wrote, "For we know in part, and we prophesy in part." Revelation after revelation, we still just know in part, amen! This revelation helps us to see more of what God sees, and will perhaps help us know how to pray for others as well. Increased knowledge helps us in so many ways.

No Perception, No Understanding

In Mark, chapter 8, verses 14–21 will be given, but only verses 17, 18, and 21 will be focused on, because of the information given in them. Jesus revealed what causes a lack of spiritual perception. Verses 14–21 state this,

> "Now the disciples had forgotten to take bread, neither had they in the ship with them more than one loaf."

> "And he charged them, saying, Take heed, beware of the leaven of the Pharisees, and of the leaven of Herod."

> "And they reasoned among themselves, saying, It is because we have no bread."

> "And when Jesus knew it, he saith unto them, Why reason ye, because ye have no bread? perceive ye not yet, neither understand? have ye your heart yet hardened?"

> "Having eyes, see ye not? and having ears, hear ye not? and do ye not remember?"

"When I brake [broke] the five loaves among five thousand, how many baskets full of fragments took ye [you] up? They say unto him, Twelve."

"And when the seven among four thousand, how many baskets full of fragments took ye up? And they said, Seven."

"And he said unto them, How is it that ye do not understand?"

We won't focus on the miracles of the loaves or the leaven, but the lack of perception of the spiritual side of things. Notice the question Jesus asked His followers in verse 21. It is a very good question about understanding spiritual things. He asked them,

"How is it that ye do not understand?"

His followers lacked understanding even after witnessing miracles and hearing Jesus preach. "How is it that" the messages of God go forth, yet there still remains such a lack of perception of spiritual things? "How is it that" God's words are proclaimed, yet there is lack of interest in what God is saying? "How is it that" the warnings of God come forth through the mouths of His servants, yet still there is lack of perception of the voice of God? "How is it that" we tell and tell about Jesus and salvation, yet there is little to no interest among many hearing? How is it?

I use to think this was due to people having a lack of the ability to discern when God communicates in the ways He does, but the Lord corrected me in this. These verses will help shed some amazing light on this subject. As God moves among us in this generation, who are they that have eyes to see, and ears to hear Him? The Bible has the answers. Looking back again at Matthew, chapter 8, verse 17, Jesus asked His followers,

"Why reason ye [you], because ye have no bread? perceive ye not yet, neither understand?"

Notice these questions asked. Do you not perceive *yet*? Do you not understand *yet*? Jesus was addressing their ability to perceive the spiritual insight. His words that follow give us an explanation to the problem of having lack of perception of spiritual things. In verse 17, Jesus asked them,

"have ye your heart yet hardened?"

There's the answer! Jesus linked the lack of perception of spiritual things to a what? A *hardened heart*, which could apparently occur even among His followers, whom He addressed, though they hadn't been baptized with the Holy Spirit at that point. A hardened heart has this effect on a person. It blocks spiritual perception. The words of Jesus in verses 17–18 reveal this fact.

"Perceive ye not yet, neither understand? have ye your heart yet hardened?"

"Having eyes, see ye not? and having ears, hear ye not? and do ye not remember?"

Read it this way, "Are you not perceiving nor understanding yet? Has your heart hardened?" A hardened heart actually prevents perception and understanding, according to Jesus. This means that if perception and understanding begins to come, there has to be a softening in the heart of a person for this to occur. In these verses Jesus mentioned perception, understanding, eyes not seeing, ears not hearing, and hardened hearts. In this we begin to see their connection with one another. Watch how the remaining verses given in this chapter confirm this truth, and bring a deeper understanding about this subject.

Stopping the Ears

In the Old Testament we can read where God mentioned the subject of non-hearing ears to His servant Ezekiel, when he was called by God to speak to the Israelites about their rebellion as a nation. As you read through these verses, notice how often God repeats the issue of Israel's rebellion. In Ezekiel, chapter 2, verses 3–5, there are details given which help to explain why ears do not hear. Verses 3–5 state,

> "And he [God] said unto me [Ezekiel], Son of man, I send thee [you] to the children of Israel, to a rebellious nation that hath rebelled against me: they and their fathers have transgressed against me, even unto this very day."

> "For they are impudent children and stiffhearted. I do send thee unto them; and thou shalt say unto them, Thus saith the Lord God."

> "And they [Israel], whether they will hear, or whether they will forbear, (for they are a rebellious house,) yet shall know that there hath [has] been a prophet among them."

In verse 3, God mentioned twice of their rebellion. In verse 4 we see He called them stiffhearted, and again in verse 5, He called them rebellious. If you read verses 6, 7, and 8, God states they were rebellious in each of those verses also. It was definitely on God's mind to express that they were—r e b e l l i o u s. I stress this fact here because God stressed it then to Ezekiel, and it will reveal something very important we should understand about rebellion. In verse 5, God said of Israel,

> "And they, whether they will hear, or whether they will forbear, (for they are a rebellious house)."

This is where the Holy Spirit drew my attention, at which time I began to get understanding about spiritual ears. Observing the words whether, will, and forbear will enlighten us to God's wisdom on this subject.

Notice God said, "whether they will hear." The word "whether" indicates hearing would be—by choice. Here are a few examples of choices using the word whether. "Whether you order salad or not," and, "Whether you bring your coat or not." Do you see how this word indicates a choice by how it's used? "Whether they will," reveals a choice being made. Also, notice that God did not say "whether they *can* hear," but "whether they will." The word "will" indicates there has to be a willingness to hear Him. Do you see that it's a choice, and a willingness?

Then we have the word forbear (KJV). The word "forbear" is translated from a word which means to cease from doing something. It means to stop, or refrain, from doing something. So, in saying "whether they will hear, or whether they will forbear," God was saying that Israel could have been willing to hear and accept His messages from Ezekiel, or they could stop the ears (forbear) from hearing. Hearing was a choice, and it was refused. This clearly reveals that hearing is absolutely a choice we have. It is the responsibility of a person to hear, and there has to be a willingness to do so. What helps to determined a willingness to hear from God is found in the next few words in verse 5:

"(for they are a rebellious house)."

The word "for" means because. If they would stop their ears to God, it was because (for) "they are...rebellious." Rebellion in the heart stops ears from hearing God, just as when children physically cover their ears at times to not hear what their parents tell them. It can be done physically, and spiritually also. If there is rebellion in the heart, the ears will not hear. Rebellion means to *turn*, or *harden* one's heart, and that being against God.

Have you ever seen someone purposely walk away from a Bible reading? Have you ever heard someone arguing with the Word? And have you ever seen someone listen to the Word with interest? People respond differently to the Word (which is Jesus), according to what is in their hearts. If a person is willing to hear what is written in the Bible, it indicates a heart that is softer toward God and His Word than the heart of someone who won't hear, and God knows this. When a person accepts the Holy Spirit, He moves in to remove the stony heart and soften it, which then becomes very willing to hear "what the Spirit saith." This is made clear in Ezekiel, chapter 2, verses 1–2. In Ezekiel,

chapter 11, verse 19, we read that God had an appointed time to give
Israel a softer heart:

> "And I will give them one heart, and I will put a new
> spirit within you; and I will take the stony heart out of
> their flesh, and will give them an heart of flesh."

Israel had a "stony heart," which is a rebellious (hard) heart. God
is the One who can remove hardheartedness from an individual. This
is what He does with His redeemed. A new Spirit is placed within
the heart of the redeemed person. It's called the seal of God. Ezekiel,
chapter 12, verse 2, offers a little more detail to look at. God again told
Ezekiel,

> "Son of man, thou dwellest [you dwell] in the midst
> of a rebellious house, which have eyes to see, and see
> not; they have ears to hear, and hear not: for they are a
> rebellious house."

Ezekiel was not rebellious, but lived among those who were. If you
will consider the fact that Ezekiel was one who heard "what the Spirit
saith." He was not in rebellion, as others were. His heart was not hard
toward God.

But notice God said that they "have eyes to see, and see not." He
said also, "they have ears to hear, and hear not." We see that they were
able to see and hear what God was saying, but didn't. Why?

> "for they are a rebellious house."

Ears that cease from hearing things pertaining to God are in
rebellion, which comes from a hard heart. I find this to be very helpful
to know. This explains the mystery of people not hearing and perceiving
things pertaining to God. This explains the mystery of why so many
turn their heads and ears from the Bible and its messages, while at the
same time many are very willing to hear. They are turning their ears
and hearts from God, and He very well knows this. Now we can know.

I have watched people respond to the Word of God and now see what God is seeing. There seems to be no reason why these people have not answered God's call, even after hearing the audible voice calling in some cases, except that they are stopping their ears to His call. I see this resistance to God. It's clearly rebellion in the heart, the place where God searches. That's why you can't force God's truth upon anyone. Forcing it does not soften their hearts, they have to choose to hear "what the Spirit saith."

I remember the time when I, at the age of 29, heard a TV evangelist three to four Sundays in a row, then quickly stood in front of the TV to pray the prayer of salvation that came at the end of the program. Tears began to surface and fall. I didn't know what was happening then, but I now know. The love of God touched me, and the seal of God came upon me. That's up to four times of hearing the gospel messages, and I had taken the bait. I have realized that some I've known have heard much more of the Gospel than I had before I was saved, yet they are not moved toward God at all. I now understand it's a condition of *hard hearts*.

Jesus stated that no one could come to Him except that God draw the person to Him (John 6:44), but when people refuse to hear about Jesus, the gospel, and salvation, it's because their ears and hearts are resistant, and God can't draw. The gospel is open to all, as is salvation, but too many don't respond. Those who look for God in everything have their spiritual ears and eyes wide open, wanting to hear and see God. They have *soft hearts*.

A Mystery behind Unbelief

The Holy Spirit recalled to me Mark, chapter 16, verses 9–14, in which it speaks of the resurrection of Jesus and the lack of belief in His followers. What the Lord led me to see was the condition of their hearts when they responded in unbelief towards the report of the event at that time. Here's more wisdom about hearts. In verses 9–11, we read,

"Now when Jesus was risen early the first day of the week, he appeared first to Mary Mag-da-le'-ne, out of whom he had cast seven devils."

"And she went and told them that had been with him, as they mourned and wept."

"And they, when they had heard that he was alive, and had been seen of her, believed not."

Mary Magdalene had seen the risen Lord. She witnessed a miracle and went to tell the others, but when her words reached their ears, there was no belief in what she had seen. None! Her testimony that God did something was rejected. Verses 12–13 state,

"After that he appeared in another form unto two of them, as they walked, and went into the country."

"And they went and told it unto the residue: neither believed they them."

Verses 12–13 reveal that others had also seen that He was alive again, and they told of their testimony. Again, the message that God had done something was rejected. That's three testimonies of the risen Christ denied as truth, by His followers. After all the miracles they saw while with Jesus, you would think they would have considered the possibility of this miracle. See here in verse 14 Jesus' response to their rejection,

"Afterward he appeared unto the eleven as they sat at meat [at the table], and upbraided them with their unbelief and hardness of heart, because they believed not them which had seen him after he was risen."

He personally appeared to them, which then gave proof of the truth of the others' testimonies. He then "upbraided them." To upbraid means to chide, to speak to in disapproval, to scold, rail, rebuke, or reprimand. To scold means to censure (blame) *severely* or *angrily*. The word reprimand is also defined as a *severe* blame for a fault. Another definition given for upbraid is to speak angrily or critically to someone concerning a wrong done. Is that clear enough? He reprimanded them about "their unbelief and hardness of heart." Here we see the Savior's disapproval of His followers' actions due to hardness of hearts, "because they believed not." When they didn't believe the miracle, there was hardness in their hearts. Jesus was, and is, not pleased with unbelief, and consider that Jesus made it known in John, chapter 14, verse 9, "He that hath seen me hath seen the Father." If it displeased Jesus, it displeased God.

Because they did not believe, they were not moved by what they had heard. "Unbelief and hardness of hearts," they are connected. This explains what we find in Revelation, chapter 21, verse 8, about the unbelieving and judgment. Here it states,

> "But the fearful, and unbelieving, and the abominable,
> and murderers, and whoremongers, and sorcerers, and
> idolaters, and all liars, shall have their part in the lake
> which burneth [burns] with fire and brimstone: which
> is the second death."

In this passage, the unbelieving are mentioned alongside the murderers, sorcerers, and idolaters. Unwilling to soften the heart, hear and believe the truth, the unbelieving will be right there with them in the lake of fire. God does not take this lightly, as we have read. Unbelief is a very serious sin, and being hardhearted is the cause. It is written in Hebrews, chapter 3, verse 12, that unbelief stems from an evil heart. Unbelief is evil to God. It's sin, and "the wages of sin is death" (Romans 6:23).

The Ears, the Eyes, and the Heart

We'll look at the Scriptures in which Jesus again spoke about the heart, concerning hearing ears and seeing eyes. Dividing these verses up in sections for pinpointing the details helps to expose more of God's wisdom on this subject. Looking again at Revelation, chapter 2, verse 23, Jesus said,

> "I am he which searcheth [searches] the reins and hearts."

The word "reins" means the minds. He searches our minds and hearts to see what is in there, whether we're aware of it or not. Proverbs, chapter 4, verse 23, says to "Keep thy heart with all diligence; for out of it are the issues of life." What's in our hearts matters, because what's in there will determine our issues, and God knows this.

Matthew, chapter 13, verses 9–15 explain much more about hearing ears and seeing eyes. These verses will help bring more clarity to the link between spiritual ears that are not hearing, and hardened hearts. We'll begin with verses 9–11 in Matthew, in which Jesus said,

> "Who hath [has] ears to hear, let him hear."

> "And the disciples came, and said unto him, Why speakest thou [you speak] unto them in parables?"

> "He answered and said unto them, Because it is given unto you to know the mysteries of the kingdom of heaven, but to them it is not given."

Notice that verse 9 reveals that Jesus called out to those who had hearing ears, and His disciples asked a very good and important question: "Why speakest thou [you speak] unto them in parables?" They wanted to know the reason for all the parables to the public. It's likely that most born again Christians have wondered about this at least once in their new life in Christ. It's written in Matthew, chapter 13, verse 34:

> "All these things spake [spoke] Jesus unto the multitude in parables; and without a parable spake he not unto them:"

Jesus spoke to the multitudes only with parables. A parable is an example used as a similarity, a likeness to something. Often enough, we read in the Scriptures that Jesus made statements such as, "The kingdom of heaven is like" (Matthew 22:2). The things of God are likened to earthly, physical things for the purpose of comparing the two. But, why doesn't God just reveal Himself to everybody? Why doesn't He just speak in plain statements that everyone can understand? Well, this is the answer He gave,

> "Because it is given unto you to know the mysteries of the kingdom of heaven, but to them it is not given."

Jesus revealed who gets to "know the mysteries" of God, and of heaven. It's His followers. Answers to the mysteries of life were and are given to those who choose Jesus, know Him, and follow His teachings. To the others, the knowledge of God and heaven remains a mystery.

Notice these words of Jesus to His followers, "it is given unto you." "The mysteries," which are the hidden things about heaven, can only come if "it is given," and that being by God. It's clearly stated by Jesus that knowledge of heaven is not given to all, but to those whom God gives it to. Those who choose to say yes to Jesus and receive the Holy Spirit will develop a relationship with Him, and in the relationship He will begin to reveal the answers to the mysteries of Him, and life. This is part of the reward for those who seek God with all their heart. The children receive the Father's knowledge. In verses 12–13 of Matthew, chapter 13, Jesus went on to say,

> "For whosoever hath [has], to him shall be given, and he shall have more abundance: but whosoever hath [has] not, from him shall be taken away even that he hath [has]."

> "Therefore speak I to them in parables: because they seeing see not; and hearing they hear not, neither do they understand."

In verse 9, Jesus began with calling out to the ears that could hear, and in verse 13, He began to reveal facts about those who do not hear spiritually. He then mentioned spiritual senses. Their physical senses of sight and hearing were working, but their spiritual sight and hearing were not. Let's now look at what Jesus said about those "who hath ears to hear," in verse 14.

> "And in them is fulfilled the prophecy of E-sa'-ias, which
> saith, By hearing ye shall hear, and shall not understand;
> and seeing ye shall see, and shall not perceive."

Jesus quoted Isaiah, chapter 6, verses 9–10, in which there is mention of seeing eyes, hearing ears, but lack of understanding. There are some very enlightening details about having ears to hear and eyes to see in verse 15, in which Jesus said this,

> "For this people's heart is waxed gross, and their ears are
> dull of hearing, and their eyes they have closed; lest at
> any time they should see with their eyes and hear with
> their ears, and should understand with their heart, and
> should be converted, and I should heal them."

Jesus mentioned three areas to be focused on: the heart, the ears, and the eyes. He explained what was happening within the people. What He said about their heart was, "For this people's heart is waxed gross." Waxing gross means to thicken, fatten, callous, or even harden. When something becomes thicker, or harder, it becomes tougher to penetrate.

To understand what happens spiritually to the heart of a person, we have to understand the term *waxed*, which is used in the King James Version. Waxing is a process of applying thin layer after thin layer of the product on something, giving it protection from, let's say, water penetration. Those thin layers add up, which give resistance to water or damaging substances. The heart also, little by little (layer by layer), becomes hardened and is difficult to penetrate with truth. The rejection of God's truth actually builds those layers of hardening, and it becomes more difficult for truth to get in. It's like a wall of resistance being built.

A good illustration are the pages of a book. They are very thin and easy to tear. But, if you close the book, all those thin pages together, layer by layer, become thick and hardened, making it difficult or impossible to tear.

Also, if you take a sharpened pencil and pierce it through one page in a book, it would go right through. But, if you close the book and try to pierce the sharp pencil through all those layers, the pencil won't pierce through. This is what takes place in the hearts of those who stop up their ears to God. Layers of hardness in the heart prevent the Word from piercing, or penetrating. Consider also that if God's truth can't pierce, a necessary transformation of the heart and mind cannot take place. So let's now see what the hardened heart causes, according to the words of Jesus. Again, verse 15 states,

> "For this people's heart is waxed gross, and their ears are
> dull of hearing, and their eyes they have closed"

Notice Jesus first mentioned the heart, then the ears and eyes. He knew and explained what we need to understand. Ears dull of hearing and spiritually closed eyes stem from hardened hearts. Look here in verse 15 and see what Jesus revealed about the eyes of the spirit:

> "and their eyes they have closed; lest at any time they
> should see with their eyes and hear with their ears."

Notice how their spiritual eyes became closed. Referring to the people whom He had spoken parables to, He said, "Their eyes they have closed." Notice who closes the eyes. People do. Jesus revealed that people are responsible for closing their spiritual eyes in saying, "they have closed." The responsibility is on the people, on us.

In 2 Corinthians, chapter 4, verse 4, it says, "The god of this world hath blinded the minds of them which believe not." Notice it says that the Devil "hath blinded the minds." This verse, if not understood, may lead us to think that the Devil is solely behind people lacking spiritual perception, but it is not so. Jesus clearly enlightens us to the fact that people can spiritually close their eyes to truth by rejecting it. If Jesus said "they have closed" their eyes, He is not accusing the Devil of this, but the people. So, how do we understand this?

Let's divide the verse up. "The god of this world hath blinded the minds." Here we read what the Devil does. He does the blinding. But, he does this to "them which believe not." If you will notice, the person is not believing. That's the sin being committed, by the person. When a person is in the sin of unbelief, the Devil will blind the mind of the one not believing. We can now understand who's doing what. God wants eyes to open and see what is going on spiritually, but when a person won't believe God's truth, the scales won't come off the eyes. Then we are given this, back in verse 15:

> "lest at any time they should see with their eyes and hear
> with their ears, and should understand with their heart,
> and should be converted, and I should heal them."

"At any time," people could choose to see and hear "what the Spirit saith," and "understand with their heart." If a person chooses to hear the Scriptures in the Bible, they are choosing to hear "what the Spirit saith," whether they are aware of it or not. It is our choice, which God told Ezekiel in saying, "whether they will." A heart that has hardened causes the spiritual ears to be dull, and the spiritual eyes to not work. They cannot sense the move of God, by choice. God's wisdom reveals it's a choice.

Be Willing to Hear

We can now understand that when Jesus called out, "Who hath ears to hear, let him hear," He was calling out to those who were and are willing to open their ears to hear Him, and His truth. See here what Jesus said, in John, chapter 5, verse 25,

> "Verily, verily, I say unto you, The hour is coming, and
> now is, when the dead shall hear the voice of the Son of
> God: and they that hear shall live."

When I heard a sister in Christ mention this verse during a teaching, the Holy Spirit immediately caught my attention on the words, "they that hear." Before Jesus went to the Cross, He said, "now is when the dead shall hear the voice of the Son of God." The dead refer those spiritually dead, not physically. The voice of the Son of God has been sounding since before He went to the Cross to sacrifice His life for us. But who will live (eternally)? "They that hear shall live," and only those who will hear "what the Spirit saith." They who do not stop up their ears, but will hear the messages. The facts are there, and the Word confirms it in more than one place.

In Isaiah, chapter 55, verse 3, it was then written that the Lord's invitation to humanity was,

> "Incline your ear, and come unto me: hear, and your soul shall live; and I will make an everlasting covenant with you."

Even in the Old Testament days, God's plea was for people to open their ears to hear Him. His desire is to "make an everlasting covenant with you." This is done through Jesus, His Son. This is the message of the gospel. Whoever accepts the gospel message and Jesus into their heart, accepts an eternal covenant with God. He wants us to hear Him.

Please note that Jesus said to those He sent out before Him into the cities, "He that heareth you heareth me" (Like 10:16). The person who hears a believer, hears Him. When we talk about salvation, those who hear us are hearing Him.

We now have a clearer understanding of why people have a difficult time hearing spiritually. It goes back to the condition of the heart. The unbelieving just plainly have a hardened heart toward God. Jesus said that at any time a person could choose to open their ears and hear, and those who do so will be awakened to the presence of the eternal God and live eternally with Him in heaven.

So, how does one begin to hear God? Being willing to listen to Bible Scriptures when they are spoken of is an act of hearing. The Bible contains the Word of God, so listening to it and accepting it is hearing God. When this is done, it shows a willingness to hear "what the Spirit saith." Just like when you speak and a person listens to your words, they are hearing you. If they turn from you, or act like they don't want to hear your words, they are forbearing.

Most importantly, verbally accepting Jesus as Lord and Savior, and receiving the Holy Spirit into the heart will give Him legal access to help you hear Him, His messages, teachings, and warnings. As mentioned previously, Ezekiel, chapter 2, verses 1–2 explain that the entering of the Holy Spirit into the heart greatly enhances the ability to hear God.

You will find other verses about hearing that may come to life now that you have enlightenment on this topic. God bless you in your studies.

Prayer

God, thank You for sending Jesus into this world to die for me,
taking the punishment for my sins on His own body on
the cross. Lord, will You help me open my eyes to see as You
see, open my ears to hear what You hear, and teach me
so that I can grow in Your knowledge and apply it in my life?
Forgive me, Lord, if I've had a hardened heart at any time in
my life toward You. Teach me to live with a soft heart toward You,
and to have faith and believe in all You want me to know
and believe. I give You thanks and glory for what You have
done and will do for me. In Jesus' name I pray, amen.

Chapter 5

Discerning the Power of Your Words

Words; we are either thinking them, or speaking them. Have you ever considered how many words you speak in a day? In a month? In a year? God gave us the ability to voice our ongoing train of thoughts. If we completely understood the effects of all our spoken words towards others, ourselves, our children, and situations, that knowledge would definitely change us. Jesus revealed a great deal about spoken words and how they affect our lives, the lives of others, living things, and also future judgment.

Within this chapter are many verses that give knowledge about spoken words, and a deeper understanding of the value of spoken words. Whether we realize it or not, all our words actually affect us throughout our lives, and will effect eternal judgment when that time arrives.

The Lord is very attentive to what words come out of the mouths of all people, especially His children. He wants His children cleaned up in word and in behavior. In the past, God began to bring my undivided attention to the words I spoke and helped my spiritual ears open to the point that I began to discern most of what I was saying. After quite some time, I realized this revelation was probably an answer to a prayer I had prayed many, many times. I often prayed for my eyes to be able to see as He sees, and my ears to hear what He was hearing. I truly desired this, and one day I began to get what I had asked for, in great detail.

At some point, God began to draw my attention on everyone's words, mine included. Almost every time people spoke around me in stores, at home, in offices, parking lots, or wherever I was, discernment of their spoken words would begin to activate, whether the words were spoken directly to me, or close enough to me that I heard them. Even my own words became a center attraction for my ears. This went on for at least a couple of years.

I came to understand this was what God was hearing, and what I heard were words of foolishness, statement after statement lacking truth (God's truth), speech containing curses, foul language, and I specifically recall much of what was heard was idle speech. There were so many statements and words discerned to be absolutely useless in speech. When words were spoken, my spiritual ears began discerning both statements, and individual words. This included words in Christian songs (discernment here was not bad), words spoken on television commercials, by people in hospitals, in stores, in conversations in the church and out, and more. This was a very enlightening two year span of my life.

Once the Holy Spirit activated this discernment, I began to hear some of what God was hearing everyday. I eventually realized, *Wow! God, You are hearing all this.* Then I began to speak up on what I was hearing, to those speaking, and some didn't respond very well, but others did. I then began to quote the words of Jesus to people: "Every idle word that men shall speak, they shall give account thereof in the day of judgment" (Matthew 12:36).

The words were coming from the hearts of the people, and I then had a better understanding about the condition of hearts and minds in this generation—just by hearing the words. Just about everything I heard spoken triggered discernment. Praise God! It's been so educational, yet alarming at the same time.

This brings me back to the days of Noah, when the great flood came as a result of the earth being filled with violence and corruption. God said, in reference to the people, that the "thought of their heart" was "only evil continually." What is in the heart comes forth out of the mouth, Scripture says. Therefore, if their thoughts were only evil, so were their words.

But the Lord is cleaning up and trying to save as many as are willing to repent and seek righteousness. I have found that when I understand my faults clearly, I'm able to repent most easily. So let's get understanding about the power of the spoken word for both God's glory, and our benefit, amen! Thank God for His mercy.

Consider and Know the
Value of Your Words

There are many Scriptures that teach about the value of spoken words. Let's begin with verses on what Jesus said concerning the words we speak. We have much to think about here in these statements He made. In Matthew, chapter 12, verses 34–37, we read that Jesus said this to the Pharisees:

> "For out of the abundance of the heart the mouth speaketh [speaks]."

> "A good man out of the good treasure of the heart bringeth [brings] forth good things: and an evil man out of the evil treasure bringeth forth evil things."

> "But I say unto you, That every idle word that men shall speak, they shall give account thereof in the day of judgment."

> "For by thy [your] words thou [you] shalt be justified, and by thy words thou shalt be condemned."

In verse 34, Jesus revealed that what is spoken out of one's mouth is what comes from the heart of a person. Keep in mind that this is the place God searches. If you want to discern what is in someone's heart, listen intently to the words they speak. If you wait on the Lord while in conversation with someone, you will be amazed at what He'll reveal to and teach you.

You might hear fear, greed, silliness, pride, lack of contentment, disbelief, insecurity, lust, hatred, or anger. On the contrary you may hear kindness, selflessness, thoughtfulness, wisdom, and so forth, by listening to the words that are spoken. When we hear in the Spirit, we hear with such greater depth of knowledge and clarity. We hear many things daily, but when these things are heard in the Spirit, it's so different.

In verse 35 above, Jesus made a distinction between "A good man," and "an evil man." He said the difference is known by *the words they speak*, from their hearts. So, Jesus knew to intently listen to the words that people spoke, because it reflected, like a mirror, what was in their hearts. This is one way in which the heart can be searched. Then He revealed this very enlightening truth in verse 36:

> "That every idle word that men shall speak, they shall
> give account thereof in the day of judgment."

Notice He mentioned "every idle word." Jesus revealed something that will take place in "the day of judgment." On the day of judgment people will have to give an account for "every idle word" they have spoken throughout their lives. Every one of them, according to this statement. An idle word is a useless, aimless, or ineffective word. To emphasize this a bit, the word every means *each one*, or *all that are possible*.

After the Holy Spirit began to teach me some of these things about words, I began telling my children to stop using the silly words and made-up syllables that made no sense. I have found that a few of the nonsense words we have used were actually either names or words in other languages.

I have done much studying on words and their origin in the past eight or more years. It's been mainly on, but not limited to, the translations of Greek and Hebrew words from the Bible. It's an amazing study. I have found that some slang words used in the south of America, Christians included, are identical to the pronunciation of words in other languages. Some are words that do not need to be spoken throughout the day, especially by Christians. For example, you may be reciting slang words in English throughout the week while pronouncing the word "sickness" repeatedly in a foreign language, without realizing it. From what I have learned, I can only assume that there are many more that I am not aware of.

After learning this about words, I discussed this with my children and explained to them that we needed to stop using what we knew to be useless words. On the day of judgment, people will stand before the Judge and give an account of a lifetime of worthless words, possibly beginning at an age of accountability. In verse 37 we read that Jesus continued to say this,

> "For by thy words thou shalt be justified, and by thy words thou shalt be condemned."

Again, notice how words will effect a person's judgment on judgment day. Jesus revealed that the spoken words of a person will be used to determine their justification, or condemnation. Isn't this interesting? Every useless word will have to be accounted for. This is basically as it is said to someone in America who is under arrest: "Anything you say may be used against you in a court of law." How amazingly similar that in judgment with God, spoken words can be used against a person. This is why God is trying to get His children to clean out their thoughts, which are spoken out of the mouth from the heart. In John, chapter 12, verses 48–49, Jesus said this about His words and judgment,

> "He that rejecteth [rejects] me, and receiveth [receives] not my words, hath [has] one that judgeth [judges] him: the word that I have spoken, the same shall judge him in the last day."

There is something very significant that is mentioned in this verse. Speaking of those who refuse Him and His words, Jesus said, "the word that I have spoken, the same shall judge him in the last day." Jesus' spoken words, which God gave Him to speak, are in the Bible. It's what we are urged by the Holy Spirit to read, study, and correct ourselves with. Correct? Jesus said, "The same [words] shall judge him." This means that whosoever does not want to hear these words and accept them now, will hear them, when they stand in judgment and are judged by them. As they are judged, they will be aware of all the moments in their life that they had rejected those very words.

The Word sits on so many bookshelves across America and is passed by perhaps for a mystery or a horror book in some stores. It's possible that the "books of the Bible" are some of the books that will be opened before the great white throne on judgment day, and there will Jesus' recorded words be, for those who refused to listen to them now. We do refer to them as books, and they do contain the Word that He has spoken. In John, chapter 12, verse 49, Jesus said,

> "For I have not spoken of myself; but the Father which sent me, he gave me a commandment, what I should say, and what I should speak."

Jesus spoke only the words that the Father gave Him to speak; therefore, it was God's wisdom Jesus gave daily. If we too wait on the Holy Spirit, He will give us words of wisdom in times of need. With the Holy Spirit as our guide, our choice of words will definitely change to be more in line with God's will for us throughout our lives.

Clarity on Curse Words: They Pierce and Destroy from Within

We find illustrations of the power of spoken words throughout the Scriptures. In the sight of His followers, Jesus did something that proved there was power in spoken words. These verses reveal the unseen damage words can cause as they are spoken, and where the destruction begins. In the following scene, Jesus and His disciples were coming from Bethany, and He was hungry. In Mark, chapter 11, verses 12–15, it states this about Jesus and a fig tree:

> "And on the morrow, when they were come from Bethany, he [Jesus] was hungry:"

> "And seeing a fig tree afar off having leaves, he came, if haply [perhaps] he might find any thing thereon: and when he came to it, he found nothing but leaves; for the time of figs was not yet."

"And Jesus answered and said unto it, No man eat fruit
of thee hereafter for ever. And his disciples heard it."

"And they come to Jerusalem."

Jesus approached a fig tree desiring some figs from it, but there were
none, because it was too early for figs. Then Jesus spoke to it. A few
verses down in this section of the Bible, Jesus taught about faith and
words in what took place with the fig tree, but we'll look into this to
see what effect words can have on a living tree, and by comparison the
human soul. Verse 13 tells us that when Jesus was looking for figs, "he
found nothing but leaves." Verse 14 then says,

"And Jesus answered and said unto it,"

Jesus said something to the tree for not having figs on it. How many
times have we ourselves been in a situation that seemed to provoke us
to speak words out loud about the inconvenience of the situation? How
many times have we spoken to an item that didn't cooperate with us in
its use? Well, Jesus chose to respond to the lack of fruit on a tree, and
His words were:

"No man eat fruit of thee hereafter for ever."

That is all He said to a living tree. These do not seem to be very
threatening words, do they? They don't seem to be disastrous words,
but God showed me something in this. Let's now go on to verses 20–21,
where they saw the fig tree the next day:

"And in the morning, as they passed by, they saw the
fig tree dried up from the roots."

"And Peter calling to remembrance saith [said] unto
him, Master, behold, the fig tree which thou cursedst
[cursed] is withered away."

In verse 20, we read that they came back to the fig tree "in the morning." It is important to understand the time span of when the tree had been spoken to, and the time the effects of the words were seen. There was a lesson in this for them then, and for us today. The tree was teeming with life the day before, but the next morning,

> "as they passed by, they saw the fig tree dried up from the roots."

Those whom Jesus was teaching (disciples) saw this tree, which was full of life only a day ago, had become lifeless "from the roots" up. It was on its way to fulfilling its God given purpose of producing fruit in its season, but one statement prevented that production, forever. See here what words such as these are called. In verse 21 it says,

> "And Peter calling to remembrance saith unto him, Master, behold, the fig tree which thou cursedst [cursed] is withered away."

Peter began to recall what took place at the fig tree the day before and put two and two together. He then spoke out to Jesus that the fig tree "which thou cursedst [cursed]" was then withered. What they saw was the result of a curse put on the tree by words spoken the previous day. All Jesus had said in verse 14 was,

> "No man eat fruit of thee hereafter forever."

That's all He said, yet those simple words had a disastrous effect on a living tree "from the roots" up. These words do not seem to be harmful, but we need to understand as God does. The words spoken to the tree were against its life. No one was going to eat fruit from it "for ever," and the tree responded with—death.

Jesus gave a very powerful example about the power of words. Its life and reason for living was destroyed because of words. The tree was dried up from the roots within a day. This reveals that those words began to destroy immediately on the inside, yet the damage it was doing was not seen until the next day, on the outside. Internally it began to malfunction, which means that things inside stopped working properly. Death came on the inside, and within a day the destruction was noticed.

Can you see the spiritual side of this? Jesus used a fruit bearing tree in this example, but consider those words being spoken to a person. Those words cursed a living thing by destroying first on the inside. The effect of words spoken against a person may not be seen immediately on the outside, but that doesn't mean the damage has not begun to take place on the inside. This simple statement against the life and production of the tree, according to Scripture, was a curse.

Curses such as this are spoken daily in society, piercing soul after soul, and God hears it. We've heard statements like this all our lives not knowing they were curses being spoken. People say things such as this to friends not realizing, according to God, they are speaking death into the ears. Consider what words you speak to your children, spouse, relatives, employees, coworkers, or anyone, because even if they are said in statements used as jokes, they could very well be curses that are doing harm that you can't see. Also, ask God to help you discern the words you are speaking, and to know which ones need to be thrown out of your vocabulary. Do not doubt that He's pleased to help us do this.

Jesus could very well have told the tree to produce edible figs, and they could have seen figs ready to eat the next morning. What He did was choose to give them, and us, an example of the powerful effect of curse words, what they are, and how they can damage a living thing.

As I was home-schooling my daughter one day, we were reading in a science book about the creation of the living creatures in the waters and the birds of the air in Genesis 1. As we were reciting Creation verses, the Holy Spirit stopped me during the reading at these words, "And God blessed them, saying...." That's when I saw blessing and cursing by words, which I'll share. The Holy Spirit prompted me to compare these words of blessing in Genesis to the words of the curse directed to the fig tree. In Genesis, chapter 1, verses 20–22, it says,

> "And God said, Let the waters bring forth abundantly the moving creature that hath [has] life, and fowl that may fly above the earth in the open firmament [sky] of heaven."

> "And God created great whales, and every living creature that moveth [moves], which the waters brought forth abundantly, after their kind, and every winged fowl after his kind: and God saw that it was good."

> "And God blessed them, saying, Be fruitful, and multiply, and fill the waters in the seas, and let fowl multiply in the earth."

The Holy Spirit showed me how He blessed the animals. In verse 22 it is written, "And God blessed them, saying...." He blessed them by "saying" *words* to them. Those words were, "Be fruitful, and multiply." That's it. In words of blessing, God spoke words that were in favor of the living creatures producing more of their kind. To this day, they keep multiplying, making more and more, fulfilling that ancient, spoken blessing. These words of blessing were spoken words that produced life. But, if you recall, Jesus spoke words that were against the tree's production, which ended its life (it produced death).

Compare God's words in Creation, "Be fruitful, and multiply," and Jesus' words to a living tree, "No man eat fruit of thee hereafter for ever." Simple words. Here we see a blessing, and a curse, both by words. Beware—God the Judge is listening.

A Piercing and a Wound

One day someone spoke something to me that God used in a very valuable lesson. As soon as those words were spoken, the Holy Spirit immediately held my attention on those words, along with an instant stir of my spirit that occurred at the very moment they were spoken. I'd never paid attention to spoken words in quite the way the Holy Spirit taught me to that day. I was able to discern unrighteous attitudes and unfit words according to the teaching of the Holy Spirit, but that day, when I heard those words, something happened in my spirit that God wanted me to learn about. He manifested at the same moment they were spoken, and I sensed a prompting to notice the stir, as if He said, "Did you feel that?"

I thought about the slight, uncomfortable stir, the words, and His presence for about half a minute. He then revealed that it was a "piercing and a wound" of the spirit. That day I began to more clearly understand how words could wound the soul. I actually felt a spiritual wound that day, as God had pointed it out for me to discern and learn from. I knew by the Holy Spirit that the words weren't spoken respectfully, and He showed me we take this way too lightly, which He does not. It is outright sin, and sin is very destructive in ways we don't understand.

The statement (words) that was spoken in a casual conversation wasn't mean or vile, but God apparently did not approve of it. God taught me a lesson that day on discerning words that pierce and wound. I have learned that not only what is spoken, but the way in which words are spoken also effect the soul, either for good or bad.

What I experienced at that moment is something that is typical and normally suppressed, because it's not recognized as a spiritual wound. If the Holy Spirit hadn't brought my attention to this, I wouldn't have recognized it. Once I understood what God revealed to me about that statement and the spiritual wound it was opening in me, He led me to consider how many times a day or a week people wound each other with words in that way. My attention then went to the wounds being made within people (not only myself) on a monthly and even a yearly basis. It was then I realized that we are literally destroying each other with our words, leaving wound after wound without realizing it.

I began to realized that this is one reason many people are in such spiritual messes. We're destroying each other with words, having no knowledge of it. There is a famine of truth in this generation. Damaging words go out, and souls become pierced. Damaging words often come from those who themselves have been wounded. It's a constant cycle. We are definitely in a wounded generation.

There is an important bit of knowledge to consider about piercing words, the example with the fig tree, and damage to the soul. The illustration with the fig tree and the next given verse both reveal the time span of a day in which damage within begins. Ephesians, chapter 4, verses 26–27, tell us, "Let not the sun go down upon your wrath," because it then gives place for the Devil (v.27) to come in and do his damage. When the sun goes down the day is over. We have until the sun goes down to resolve any anger issue and wounds we may have from it. If it is not dealt with and released within the day, that means the sun has gone down on our wrath. We are warned that the Devil is then given a place to move in, bound us up in the anger, and destroy within as he is able.

The point here is that within a day the fig tree showed the awful effects of words spoken against it, and within a day anger and its wounds have to be released, or spiritual damage will begin. If we are aware of a spiritual hurt, a wound, then we need to quickly forgive, resolve the matter and clean the wound, or watch out, because spiritual damage will come otherwise.

Destructive words go into the soul and cause harm within, bringing destruction to God's creation. According to Scripture, Jesus' words were a curse, which harmed the tree and brought death. It's a very powerful illustration. Our souls are affected by, and respond to, words spoken. Proverbs, chapter 18, verse 21, states,

> "Death and life are in the power of the tongue: and they
> that love it shall eat the fruit thereof."

Notice that both "death and life are in the power of the tongue." As we begin to speak, the little tongue starts to move and form words that have power. We can speak things that produce death, or learn to speak words that produce life, which is God's will. According to these words, the tongue has tremendous power, and Jesus showed us this with the fig tree He spoke to. To this we can add the words in 1 Peter, chapter 3, verse 10:

> "For he that will love life, and see good days, let him
> refrain his tongue from evil, and his lips that they speak
> no guile."

This again addresses the powerful effect of words that are spoken. Our words affect our lives in such a way that if we want to love life with good days, learning to control the words we speak is a great and necessary benefit. Refraining from speaking evil things will actually bring goodness into one's life. So, the condition of our lives has something to do with our language, or speech, according to this verse. This is God's hidden wisdom, which He inspired to be written so that we can learn this. Another verse containing knowledge about spoken words is Proverbs, chapter 18, verse 7, which states,

"A fool's mouth is his destruction, and his lips are the snare of his soul."

Again, the use of the mouth is addressed. What we speak can bring trouble and destruction into our own lives. There is a clear connection given here between a troubled soul and the words spoken from that soul. The way in which we speak and communicate in life very much affects our lives. It also affects the condition of both our own souls, and the souls of others. The damaging words of others can harm our souls if we don't forgive others and release those issues to God, but our own words need to be evaluated also. A person who doesn't have this wisdom will reap the destruction from the evil fruit of their lips, and have no clue as to why they are reaping what they are. It's termed as "a fool's mouth." But let us be wise in the Lord, and share this knowledge. I would love to have had this knowledge imparted to me much earlier in my life. Here in Proverbs, chapter 16, verse 24, it actually reveals that there is a healing power in good righteous speech. It says,

"Pleasant words are as an honeycomb, sweet to the soul, and health to the bones."

This is so opposite from what has been presented so far. "Pleasant words" have something to do with good health. Pleasant words cause our souls to respond in pleasure and delight. They are sweet, and our soul delights in them. So, if pleasant words bring "health to the bones," then unpleasant words bring troubles within.

Challenge yourself today to begin saying some amazingly pleasant words to people, and perhaps yourself, and recognize your soul's peaceful response to this change. Observe others' response to your words throughout the day also. I recall this was a challenging process for me. Trying to subject my mouth was a big task. As the Holy Spirit revealed knowledge on this subject in the process of changing my speech, the change became inviting. I rather enjoyed the righteous change, though I've had my share of mess-ups. Righteousness is actually attractive.

Not only does our speech affect our lives, it can and does affect those around us, tremendously. When you wake up and begin your day, remember that your words truly are powerful. Proverbs, chapter 21, verse 23, says,

> "Whoso keepeth [keeps] his mouth and his tongue keepeth his soul from troubles."

Here again it shows the connection between troubles in our souls and the way we speak. The word "keep" in this verse is from the Hebrew word *shamar*, which means to watch over the mouth. It also means to tend to or hedge the mouth, as if to guard it. The message in this is to be on guard and watch what we speak. Have you ever heard a parent tell their child, "watch your mouth"? Well, God says this too. If we discipline ourselves in what we say and how we say it, we will encounter less troubles in life. How does that sound? If we reap what we sow, as Scripture reveals, then disastrous words will reap disasters, and righteous words will reap righteousness.

People today have many troubles, and Scripture reveals that it's partly because of what and how we speak. We can't control what everyone else speaks, but we should learn to watch our own words, because God hears, and they can bring death or life.

Some good educational facts about the way we speak our words are in Proverbs, chapter 15, verse 1. God used this verse in teaching me not to speak with angry words. Having had anger within me, angry words often came out of me. Once I had a clear understanding of what this verse taught, I became aware of the fact that I needed to begin changing my words, and gain control of what and how I spoke. Proverbs, chapter 15, verse 1, says,

"A soft answer turneth [turns] away wrath: but grievous words stir up anger."

"Grievous words stir up anger." Grievous words are bad, severe, harsh, or bitter words. Harsh means to cause discomfort or pain. When "grievous words" are spoken, they stir anger in people. Grievous words cause pain and discomfort in the soul. Actually, this is what feeling the Holy Spirit pointed out to me during the lesson previously mentioned concerning the "piercing and a wound."

When I was in the sin of bitterness, I spoke grievous words, but didn't know it. It wasn't until I gave my life to Jesus that I began to recognized this sin issue. After reading this verse several times, God began to teach me about it. He showed me that I was doing this stirring.

While in the midst of saying harsh words in past times, God would began to draw my attention to my words, and the stirring. As I would realize what I was doing, I would begin to back off from doing it. After many times of being stopped in the midst by God, I learned to notice it myself and stop. When I was able to recognize that I was doing this stirring, I was ready to stop it. What I experienced was less troubles for my soul. It's amazing and true that when I fixed me, I had more peace within. It is a case of gaining self control through God's wisdom.

On the contrary, when soft words are spoken they can turn away anger. Soft words are opposite of grievous words. Have you ever heard of someone being "soft-spoken"? They speak soft words. Grievous words stir up anger, but soft words turn it away. I've tested this in the past and still do today, and yes, it works. Hallelujah! Soft words are actually more pleasant to the ear. Grievous words are an irritant to the ear.

Learn to Control the Little Mouth

James, chapter 3, verses 2-10, also reveal some very interesting, additional facts about how and what we speak. Verse 1 warns of the strict judgment those who teach will be under, because much knowledge is given to those who study and teach. Teachers have the responsibility to impart their knowledge to others and are to practice what they teach, being an example of what doing the Word looks like. Concerning the words we speak, verse 2 reads,

> "For in many things we offend all. If any man offend not in word, the same is a perfect man, and able also to bridle the whole body."

"We offend all" means that we all stumble or sin in many ways. According to this verse, "a perfect man" is one who speaks without offending others "in word." When we are able to discipline ourselves in our speech, then self-control of the "whole body" can be achieved, or is likely in the process of being achieved. The whole body is able to come under subjection if and when the little mouth is controlled. But how is this?

View it this way. If our speech reflects our thoughts, then changing the way we think will naturally change our speech. Also, if our actions are a reflection of our thoughts, then changing our thoughts will naturally change our actions (behavior). Therefore, as our thoughts change, both our speech and behavior will change. This is as it says in Proverbs, chapter 23, verse 7, saying, "For as he thinketh in his heart, so is he." We are the way we think. This is some of God's hidden wisdom. This is why God says to renew the mind (Romans 12:2). God teaches us to think differently using His Word.

"If any man offend not in word, the same is a perfect man." The word *perfect* here is from the Greek word *teleios,* which means being mature both mentally and morally. It also means completeness. Learning to control the way in which we speak indicates a higher level of maturity. According to this verse, one who is considered perfect or complete will sin less in words. Can you see the importance of learning to discern and control what we speak? All is possible with God. In 1 Peter, chapter 2, verses 22–23, Peter wrote this about Jesus,

> "Who did no sin, neither was guile found in his mouth."

> "Who, when he was reviled, reviled not again; when
> he suffered, he threatened not."

Jesus, being perfect, did not offend with His words. He did not turn on people with His words when they reviled Him. As He suffered, He did not threaten anyone with words. He did speak truth though, which stirred the souls of many. Scripture reveals that He spoke only what God told Him to speak. The Holy Spirit recalled to me the writings of Job concerning this topic. In the first two chapters of Job it reveals the evil that came into his life. In chapter 2, verse 7, it reveals that Satan attacked Job in his body, attempting to get him to turn against God. But in verse 10 it says this about Job,

> "In all this did not Job sin with his lips."

God allowed Satan to attack Job and test his loyalty to Him. In his sufferings, Job did not "sin with his lips." To sin means to stumble or offend. In chapter 1, verse 1, it is written that Job was a "perfect and upright" man. The word "perfect" in this verse is from the Hebrew word *tam,* which also means complete. He was a man of complete maturity who offended not "in word," as was mentioned in James chapter 3, verse 2. Job did not sin and turn against God with his words, though Satan tried to get him to do so.

The ability to control what we speak indicates an ability to control self. Looking back in James, chapter 3, verse 3, it goes on to say,

> "Behold, we put bits in the horses' mouths, that they
> may obey us; and we turn about their whole body."

In this wonderful illustration, we are reminded that the entire body of a horse can be guided and turned by using its mouth. Verse 4 gives another illustration:

> "Behold also the ships, which though they be so great,
> and are driven of fierce winds, yet are they turned about
> with a very small helm, whithersoever the governor
> listeth."

"Whithersoever the governor listeth," means "wherever the pilot wants to go." Compared to a ship, a helm is very small, yet it can turn the whole course of the ship. These are very good examples that help explain the effect of the little mouth on the entire body. A simple bit can turn a big horse, a small rudder can turn a huge ship, and the small mouth can change the course of our lives. Verses 5–6 then say,

> "Even so the tongue is a little member, and boasteth great things. Behold, how great a matter a little fire kindleth!"

> "And the tongue is a fire, a world of iniquity: so is the tongue among our members, that it defileth [defiles] the whole body, and setteth [sets] on fire the course of nature; and it is set on fire of hell."

"The tongue is a fire." Small fires can expand and travel for miles leaving a path of total destruction and devastation behind it, if it's not brought under control and extinguished quickly. It can and does destroy lives. Likewise, the little tongue that God has given us, if not controlled, can cause a great deal of destruction in our lives. It can actually determine the course of our lives, according to what is given in this verse. Isn't this enlightening? Our little mouths can determine the condition of path we take. Our hearts play a role in this because we only speak what is in our hearts. When the hearts are transformed, the speech will also be transformed. The heart is where God wants in, so that He can do some amazing transformations. In verse 6, again we read,

> "And the tongue is a fire, a world of iniquity: so is the tongue among our members, that it defileth the whole body, and setteth [sets] on fire the course of nature; and it is set on fire of hell."

There is much to consider in this verse. These are words of warning. In this we also read of the tongue, "it defileth the whole body." If what is spoken is corrupt, it can blemish the whole person. Imagine every part of you being dirty in God's eyes as a result of the words you use.

Without getting into detail, I specifically remember two times that God stopped me immediately when speaking harmful words. This was when I was basically a "babe in Christ," not being a very mature Christian. During a couple of times when others had angered me, with their words in one case, and actions in another case, I spoke out words in anger that were apparently not acceptable to the Holy Spirit. I knew because I immediately sensed His presence right next to me while receiving very clearly—"take it back now!" The first time it frightened me somewhat, because suddenly, "there was God." He was no longer a mystery at that moment, but was in my car hearing me. I didn't intend harm with my words, but I was very angered and wounded by the careless words of another.

In both cases the other parties were not righteous in their behavior and words, but being in God's kingdom, my behavior was not acceptable to a righteous King. We have to learn to do His will no matter what anyone else does, or says. I began to get unforgettable lessons such as these, but I am very thankful. I am able to know Him, learn His will, and prepare for eternity with Him by learning about Him.

"The tongue...setteth on fire the course of nature; and it is set on fire of hell" (v. 6). James clearly makes it known that the mouth which speaks destructively is associated with the location of hell, in the depths below. What most of the world does not realize is that we have two spiritual influences that can affect our behavior in life: the Devil and his kingdom, or Jesus and His kingdom. In John, chapter 8, verses 42–47, Jesus made this very clear. When details of this are understood, much in life can better be understood.

When we accept God's truth and His Son Jesus Christ, it is then that Jesus Himself steps in and begins to influence and guide us out of destructive behavior. We may think our behavior is okay, but when God shows us what He sees, and teaches us what He knows, we get a good glimpse of what our natural behavior is truly like—it's very unholy.

What we speak actually affects our lives in ways we have not understood. Keep in mind the illustration of the words spoken by Jesus to the fig tree. Destruction came to the tree. Destruction means to ruin or damage. Destructive words ruin relationships with spouses, children, and friends, bringing damage to the relationships. Destructive words can cause job loss. Words are powerful, either for good or evil.

"The tongue is a fire," and we need to learn to extinguish the corrupt speech while allowing Jesus to help us produce a good profitable speech or vocabulary. Jesus will honor the change and bring the blessings. Who in there right mind wants to look back in life and see a trail of destruction that has followed? Too many of us have had that trail of destruction in our past that we look back to, or know that it was there. Not that we are to dwell on it, but it's there with its lessons. It reminds us where we've come from. Verses 7–8 tell us,

> "For every kind of beast, and of birds, and of serpents, and of things in the sea, is tamed, and hath been tamed of mankind:"

> "But the tongue can no man tame; it is an unruly evil, full of deadly poison."

Apparently, it's more difficult to control what comes out of the mouth than it is to control serpents and animals, but the Bible says all things are possible with God. Verse 8 states the tongue is "full of deadly poison." Remember that Jesus spoke words to the fig tree and it died, as if it were poisoned. We now move into verses 9–10, which say,

> "Therewith bless we God, even the Father; and therewith curse we men, which are made after the similitude of God."

> "Out of the same mouth proceedeth blessing and cursing. My brethren, these things ought not so to be."

James pointed out the fact that with the same mouth blessings go to God, and curses go forth to people. Blessing God is good. Cursing mankind is not, but people are using their mouths to do this while not realizing it. The message here is that we need to recognize corrupt speech and turn from it. "Every idle word that men shall speak, they shall give account thereof in the day of judgment," warns Jesus. We better make our words profitable. Growth in knowledge transforms us if we use the knowledge, and God has plenty to share with us.

Luke, chapter 18, verse 27, says, "The things which are impossible with men are possible with God." With God it is possible for us to change in all areas in our lives, which is a requirement of God. "Be ye transformed," He says (Romans 12:2). To say we can't would be calling God a liar, being we just read of the possibility of it happening only with Him. It takes two things for change: a willing heart, and the move of the Holy Spirit. Philippians, chapter 4, verse 13, tells us, "I can do all things through Christ which strengthenth [strengthens] me." All these things can be done through Jesus Christ alone.

Without Him we don't even know what or how we are to change. Actually, without Him we don't know what we are doing wrong to know we need to change. Through Jesus Christ we can change our words, heart, thoughts, and course of life, if desired. Jesus will lead us to change, which will bring the peace of God within; a peace that is beyond any peace we have ever known in our hearts. We should not reject this from God.

Who would not want peace and rest within the soul from the stresses and issues encountered in this generation? A change within will have to take place for this to happen. Are you ready to begin decreasing the troubles in your soul? The Holy Spirit wants to come in and help. Jesus said He will give rest to your soul (Matthew 11:29–30). For a new life that leads to better speech and rest within, pray these prayers out loud to God. May the Lord bless you, and keep you.

Prayer for Salvation

God, I believe in You, and I believe Jesus was Your
Son who took the punishment for my sins
when He died on the cross. Will You forgive me for
my sins, come into my heart, baptize me with Your
Holy Spirit, and save me? Today, I confess Jesus as my
Lord and Savior. In Jesus' name I pray, amen.

Prayer for Words of Wisdom

Lord, I understand that my words are valuable and that
Your will is for my words to be wise, not destructive.
Your Word says that if we need wisdom, all we have to do
is ask for it, and You will freely give it. Lord, will You
give me wisdom to live by? Teach me to discern destructive
words, and to speak with words of wisdom. Thank
You for hearing my request. In Jesus' name I pray, amen.

Chapter 6

Casting Stones of Judgment

In this chapter is a study about judgment. It's based on a revelation given about the situation with the stones that were about to be thrown at a woman who was caught committing adultery in the days that Messiah had come to take away our sins. I'll show through Scripture how the Holy Spirit leads us to judge ourselves, which is His will. Jesus made it clear that we should "judge righteous judgment" in life (see John 7:24). Learning to judge matters and situations in life with wisdom is God's desire for us. This would involve examining matters, situations, or circumstances and making decisions accordingly. But this study is on what God says about people condemning others for their sins, and judgment on self.

The word *judge* means to make a decision, to try, examine, condemn, or punish. It also means to form an opinion on. It's easy to see others' faults, but it's not so easy to perceive our own. We are a spirit, having a soul and a body. From a spiritual perspective, we are always on the inside looking out at others, therefore we don't see and observe ourselves as well as we do others. Is it okay that we look at and judge others throughout our lives? No. God wants us to stop looking so much at the sins of others at this time, and learn to recognize our own sins. There are very important reasons why God wants us to learn self-judgment now, and the Scriptures given will explain why.

Recognizing sin in others is not wrong. It's very beneficial to be able to recognize sin in ourselves, and in this world. It is a blessing to be able to recognize the rise of sin in a nation, because it allows one to know what is happening, and what is going to happen, such as judgment. God doesn't want us ignorant of sin, but righteous judgment is desired by God from us.

Included in this chapter are many verses that reveal many, very interesting facts about judging. This is God's wisdom freely given to us. In this study is a focus on Scriptures that mention judging others, and their given details. Also, there is a very good illustration in the Bible that is given to show how God, through Jesus, helped some people judge themselves while they were focusing on the sin of another.

Within this chapter are also some verses that help us understand how self-judgment will play an important role in the coming kingdom of Jesus Christ, and with those who inherit that kingdom.

Beware of Judging Others

Concerning judging other people, Romans, chapter 2, verses 1–3, inform us of what might be indicated when a fault is found in another. These verses help us to see that while focusing intently on the sins of others, we are likely doing the same things. The apostle Paul said,

> "Therefore thou art [you are] inexcusable, O man, whosoever thou art that judgest [judges]: for wherein thou judgest another, thou condemnest thyself [you condemn yourself]; for thou [you] that judgest doest the same things."

> "But we are sure that the judgment of God is according to truth against them which commit such things."

> "And thinkest thou [do you think] this, O man, that judgest them which do such things, and doest [do] the same, that thou shalt [you shall] escape the judgment of God?"

Paul made it clear in his rebuke that day, "For wherein thou judgest another, thou condemnest [you condemn] thyself." This means that in judging another for their faults (sins), the one judging is actually bringing awareness to their own guilt without realizing it. How is this? When sin in another is noticed, we often mentally (or verbally) judge the wrong in it. Lacking knowledge, the one judging "doest the same things," said Paul. Therefore, if detected as wrong in another and you are committing the same sin in some way, you have just declared yourself guilty of a wrong that you are not yet aware of. It's self-condemnation.

Moreover, of the one who judges it says, "And thinkest thou [do you think] this...that thou shalt escape the judgment of God?" Paul warned that there is no escape from God's judgment while being guilty of the same crime that you have judged in another. No escape.

Was this the issue only of whom Paul addressed, or could this be the case for all people in general? Could anyone finding fault in another be just as guilty of the same fault? According to these words, anyone who is judging another is most likely to be guilty in some way of the very same thing that he or she sees in and judges another for. This may not be specific in every case, which will be seen in later verses, but Scripture does reveal that we are most likely guilty of doing what we detect in others. So, beware!

While going through this study, God began to show me how people judge in their thoughts, voice the complaint of it, and are just as guilty without realizing it. From what the Holy Spirit has shown me, we all seem to do this. After pulling all these verses together, the Holy Spirit began to reveal something during my conversations with others. As I was hearing some complaints from people about others, I was amazed as the Holy Spirit led me then to realize the exact ways in which the accuser was doing the same thing he or she was accusing another of. The *exact* same ways.

In the conversations, the Holy Spirit would begin bringing to mind the same errors of the accuser. As my physical ears heard the person speak, the Lord opened my understanding and brought to mind the ways in which the accuser was doing the same. The evidence was there. The Holy Spirit pointed this out for me to comprehend the reality of what these verses say. It is exactly as Paul said.

On another day, I heard another's verbal judgment on a person in a news report. As the last couple of words of the judgment came out their mouth, the Holy Spirit immediately showed me in a vision their own guilt and judgment, which was *identical* to the judgment they had just cast on the one they had judged. God was there listening, and responded to what He had heard. God revealed at other times where judging and guilt of the same was taking place, and I began to realize—we are all doing this.

As God revealed more about how people judge in this way, while being guilty themselves of the same, I began to see the truth of this Scripture right before my eyes. I began to realize I was probably doing this too. This revelation caused me to start seriously evaluating my own ways. Knowing what I then knew, I began to examine myself as the Holy Spirit led. Not only was I given understanding about these Scriptures, He showed me the reality of it in life today. I realized that this Scripture means exactly what it says.

One revelation I received from God was about my own ways. As I was considering the ways of someone else one day, the Holy Spirit, knowing my thoughts, recalled a time when I didn't care for the way in which I'd been addressed by others about issues I'd had before I was born into God's family. Yet, there I was similar in my ways of addressing faults of others. That's when I was shown my own guilt. After realizing it, I could then begin to pray and change in me what I didn't like. Without the Holy Spirit, I would not have recognized it to repent of it.

The fact is, we judge others being guilty in some way of the same faults and don't even realize it. The sin looks so bad on others, and we don't realize that at the same time it's looking just as bad on us. It's difficult to see our own sins, but the Holy Spirit delights in helping us to see them, and lead us out of them. We should ask the Lord to show us our sins and proceed to judge ourselves.

If you do happen to notice that you are judging someone, stop and ask God, "am I also doing that Lord?" You may not be, but it's likely that you are. When your judgment is turning on yourself, that is what God wants. It's better to learn to judge ourselves than to keep taking notice of and judging the ways of others, while criticizing our own unknown sins. Romans chapter 2, verse 4, says,

> "Or despisest thou [do you despise] the riches of his goodness and forbearance and longsuffering; not

> knowing that the goodness of God leadeth thee [leads
> you] to repentance?"

When we have come to a place where we are prepared to turn
from our faults, it's God who has led us to that point. It's God who
"leadeth thee to repentance." He wants to lead us out of sin, including
unrighteous judgment. When I realized I was guilty of some things I
was judging others for, it was a very enlightening experience. I began
to realize how ridiculous I looked in God's sight. Change then becomes
very inviting. Self-judgment is a beneficial level to be at, and it's very
rewarding. When your own sins become as evident as the sins of others,
and conviction arises, it's an indication that the Holy Spirit is leading
you into self-judgment for the purpose of self-cleaning. He wants us
to be able to judge ourselves, and there are some amazing reasons why.

Being a mother of three, and having had them each seven years
apart, I was delighted when my third child began to microwave pizza
rolls and fix a bowl cereal on her own. Her growth and independence
I have welcomed, just as God must be pleased when we, His children,
learn to do on our own what He spends so much time teaching us,
including judging ourselves.

Jesus Warns Us to Judge Ourselves

After we learn to judge ourselves, we are more able to help others
remove what the Bible refers to as logs, splinters, twigs, motes, and
other debris—sin—out of their eyes. These are symbolic terms that
Jesus used when preaching about the hypocrisy of trying to help others
remove their sins, and not first tending to our own. God doesn't oppose
our helping others with sin issues, but let's first fix ourselves and be
prepared to help others.

In Matthew chapter 7, verses 1–6, Jesus revealed a mystery about
judging others, ourselves, and how God judges. This insight is truly
amazing! What He spoke explains how judgment occurs, when it's
likely to occur, to what extent, and most important, *how we may avoid it.*
There is an abundance of wisdom to be gained within these statements.

He also revealed how we can spiritually see more clearly. In Matthew, chapter 7, beginning with verse 1, Jesus said,

"Judge not, that ye [you] be not judged."

Jesus informed His disciples that they should "judge not," and the reason given was, "that ye be not judged." Do you see what this is saying? We should not judge others so that we ourselves won't be judged. This is judgment prevention. According to this verse, judging others will lead us into a judgment—from God. Therefore, Jesus said not to judge so that we won't encounter judgment. Jesus did not withhold this information; He revealed it, and now we have it.

This is what the apostle Paul was referring to back in Romans chapter 2, verse 3, when he said that the one judging another's sins, while being guilty of the same sins, would not escape from being judged by God. If we judge and are guilty ourselves, then judgment is coming our way; there's no escaping. The following verses will help in understanding more about this. So, "judge not, that ye [you] be not judged." Moving into verse 2 of Matthew 7, Jesus further said,

"For with what judgment ye [you] judge, ye [you] shall be judged: and with what measure ye mete, it shall be measured to you again."

Jesus mentioned two things to focus on in this verse: a judgment, and a measure. If we move these words around without changing any meaning, we can read it this way, "Ye shall be judged" "with what judgment ye judge." The word judgment used here is from the Greek word *krima*, which means a decision, or a sentence pronounced. So let's say it this way, in hopes of getting better understanding about judgment: "With what sentence you pronounce on another, you will be sentenced." We will be judged with the degree of judgment we judge others by. Jesus revealed that if we are to avoid this, don't judge.

I think of it this way, if my Lord will judge me with a degree of judgment that I am casting on others, it seems best if I learn not to judge others, because He's watching. Understanding this helped me to stop, mainly in my thoughts, being so critical of others' faults and consider if I was doing the same. This is more of God's hidden wisdom. Praise God! Verse 2 then says,

> "and with what measure ye mete, it shall be measured
> to you again."

The words "ye mete" means "you measure." The *measure of judgment* you use to judge others, Jesus said, "shall be measured to you again." Do you see here what Jesus revealed? The extent or intensity (amount) of judgment we judge others with is the extent or intensity used to measure back judgment upon us, or the one judging.

Again, if one judges, then he or she *will be judged*. They will be judged in the *same judgment* they have judged another. Also, the amount of judgment used is measured and used back in judgment, on the one who has judged. The same judgment, and the same measure. So let's learn not to judge.

In Luke, chapter 6, verses 37–38, he also stated these words of Jesus, but also mentioned that if we forgive, we will also be forgiven. It is actually the case of reaping *exactly* what we sow, as mentioned in Galatians, chapter 6, verse 7, saying, "Be not deceived; God is not mocked: for whatsoever a man soweth, that shall he also reap." If we sow judgment, we reap judgment, and in the same amount.

Throughout the Bible, it's written that God rewards humanity *according to* their deeds, good or bad. This means it's measured back, good or bad. If I intensely judge others, I can expect intense judgment from God (now that I am aware of this). If I cast no judgment upon others, God will not judge me.

But God desires that we learn to judge ourselves so all this measuring back again will be avoided. In Hosea, chapter 4, verse 6, God said, "My people are destroyed for lack of knowledge." We now have His knowledge on how He judges. We now know how God measures judgment and can better understand verses such as Revelation, chapter 16, verse 7, which says,

> "Lord God Almighty, true and righteous are thy
> judgments."

This verse refers to the judgment of the third vial (bowl) of God's wrath that will come upon earth in the days of tribulation. This judgment is rivers and fountains turning bloody, because "the blood of saints and prophets" will have been shed (Revelation 16:6). The judgment that will come to those killing God's people will be judgment that will have been *measured back* to them: blood for blood, exact measurement. We can understand that if judgment has come, or is coming, it has been or will be—*measured*. I have sometimes wondered about the measure that Satan is going to get. Moving on into verse 3 of Matthew, chapter 7, Jesus said,

> "And why beholdest thou the mote [a twig] that is in
> thy brother's eye, but considerest not the beam [the log]
> that is in thine own eye?"

Jesus addressed this issue in the form of a question: "Why do you do this?" "You see your brother's little faults, but you are not considering your own." The word "mote" is understood to be a small, dry branch, or a piece of dried stem, such as straw. Jesus addressed the fact that the sin (small twig) in others may seem noticeable to us to the point that we want to pull it out of them and help clean up their personality, but our own sin (beam) could very well be larger in comparison, and first needs to be considered and removed.

The beams and motes and the logs and twigs mentioned refer to sin in one's life. It is mentioned being in the eye because having something in the eye obstructs the sight, as does sin. Disturbing traits that we see in others may possibly be pale in comparison to the sin we are exhibiting. What's the solution to this dilemma? In verses 4–5, Jesus said,

> "Or how wilt thou [will you] say to thy brother, Let me
> pull out the mote out of thine [your] eye; and, behold,
> a beam is in thine own eye?"

> "Thou [you] hypocrite, first cast out the beam out of
> thine [your] own eye; and then shalt thou [you] see
> clearly to cast out the mote out of thy brother's eye."

We should know that Jesus labeled this as being a hypocrite. I'd prefer that Jesus did not look upon me and think this way of me. Do you? He says, "first cast out the beam out of thine [your] own eye." The "beam" in the eye is the sin that blinds our perception, and it should be dealt with and removed, and then we read,

"then shalt thou [shall you] see clearly."

This bit of knowledge is so enlightening, and good for us to understand. What we are given from Jesus is to "first cast out the beam [sin] out of thine own eye." Self evaluation (judgment) and repentance should come first. Taking the time to be led by the Holy Spirit to repentance is important. What results from this is, "then shalt thou see clearly." When we are full of sins, we don't see too clearly. To see more clearly, sins have to be removed.

For example, if you lived on the south side of a forest, your view to what was on the north side of the forest would be very limited, or blocked, because of the trees (beams of wood). If that forest were to be cleared tree by tree (beam by beam), your view to what is on the north side would become clearer as the trees in the forest were removed. If the entire forest was cleared, it would be then you would have a clear view of what's in the direction of the north. You would then see clearly.

Jesus was sin free; how clearly He saw in everyone. Those who are purged from many sins will see more clearly than the babes in Christ who are yet to be purged. Sin blocks our perception of spiritual truth. As God helps remove the sin of those believing in Jesus, spiritual perception grows clearer and clearer, and "then shalt thou [shall you] see clearly to cast out the mote out of thy brother's eye" (v. 5). If we want to help others get free of spiritual problems or sin, we should let the Holy Spirit help us clear out our beams of sin so we can see more clearly to help others effectively.

Paul Said We Should Judge Ourselves

In 1 Corinthians, chapter 11, verses 31–32, the apostle Paul wrote some facts about judging ourselves also, and the consequences of not doing so. He basically stated what Jesus said, because his teaching came from Jesus. This is where the Holy Spirit began to hold my attention on things concerning judgment, and helped me piece some of this knowledge together. I suggest you read the verses that surround these verses to learn what Paul was teaching, but only these will be studied for added details about judgment. In 1 Corinthians, chapter 11, verses 31–32, Paul said,

> "For if we would judge ourselves, we should not be judged."

> "But when we are judged, we are chastened of the Lord, that we should not be condemned with the world."

There is much knowledge to be gained within these two verses. Remember Jesus stated that we will be judged with what judgment we judge others. Is this referring to believers also? Well, please note that Paul said "we" in these verses, which means he included himself concerning this knowledge. Paul said in the beginning of verse 31, "For if we would judge ourselves, we should not be judged." Mentioned previously, this is what Jesus taught (Matthew 7:1): "Judge not, that ye be not judged." Paul added that we should not only keep from judging others, but turn the judgment on ourselves. If we let the Lord teach us how to judge ourselves, then "we should not be judged." How enlightening!

The wisdom we find in these statements is that if we can get to the level of judging ourselves regularly, we won't have to be judged by God. Hallelujah! Yes, we can learn to do judgment, yet on ourselves. Scripture suggests we do so for our benefit. In verse 32, he further said,

> "But when we are judged, we are chastened of the Lord, that we should not be condemned with the world."

If we do not recognize our own sins and change, we'll be judged by the One who is saving us. "But when we are judged, we are chastened of the Lord." From this we can know and understand that when we, the children of God, are judged, "we are chastened." This is defined as training or educating us, by what ever means He does so. God is actually educating those whom He chastens, His children; *disciplining* is another word for chastening. So, God does chasten His children when He judges them, to educate, train and discipline them.

The purpose in God judging the redeemed is so that "we should not be condemned with the world," according to Paul. Yes, this is what it's telling us. You may think, "Well, there's 'no condemnation to them which are in Christ Jesus'" (Romans 8:1). I've quoted this myself so many times, and for many years. But, we can't assume that Paul was crazy, and that he didn't know what he was talking about. He was divinely inspired, according to what he had said. The verse in Romans continues to say, "who walk not after the flesh, but after the Spirit." There's the catch. There's no condemnation to those who walk "after the Spirit," he said. The message here is to learn to walk "after the Spirit," and get out of the flesh.

God is trying to get the sin out, so it's best if we learn to judge ourselves rather than spend time judging others. When I began learning to stop judging others, it truly freed my mind from much time wasted on doing this. I could then spend that time on evaluating myself. I'm thankful.

God Helped Them Judge Themselves

Now we'll look at some verses written about a situation concerning adultery, and notice some more valuable details on the subject of judging others. We will see how the God of Creation handled a situation in which people wanted to punish another for their sin. This is where we get to see God lead people into self-judgment. This has definitely helped me to see what God wants from us. Please understand that adultery is sin, and we do need to understand the difference between what is good and what is evil in the eyes of God. Sin is not to be taken lightly. The lake of fire awaits the unrepentant. But it seems that as God ushered in the new covenant, the responsibility to evaluate right and wrong within ourselves came with it. God says that vengeance is His, and He means it. In John, chapter 8, verses 1–11, it describes the scene of a woman guilty of adultery, and men guilty of other things:

"Jesus went unto the mount of Olives."

"And early in the morning he came again into the temple, and all the people came unto him; and he sat down, and taught them."

"And the scribes and Pharisees brought unto him a woman taken in adultery; and when they had set her in the midst,"

"They say unto him, Master, this woman was taken in adultery, in the very act."

"Now Moses in the law commanded us, that such should be stoned: but what sayest thou [do you say]?"

"This they said, tempting him, that they might have to accuse him. But Jesus stooped down, and with his finger wrote on the ground, as though he heard them not."

"So when they continued asking him, he lifted up himself, and said unto them, He that is without sin among you, let him first cast a stone at her."

"And again he stooped down, and wrote on the ground."

"And they which heard it, being convicted by their own conscience, went out one by one, beginning at the eldest, even unto the last: and Jesus was left alone, and the woman standing in the midst."

"When Jesus had lifted up himself, and saw none but the woman, he said unto her, Woman, where are those thine [your] accusers? hath [has] no man condemned thee?"

"She said, No man, Lord. And Jesus said unto her, Neither do I condemn thee [you]: go, and sin no more."

Now we will look back at selected areas of these verses to understand what was done in this situation. In this scene, we actually see self-judgment being enforced, or rather prompted, by the Holy Spirit. It is very enlightening when we are able to take our focus off the scenes of the Scripture and put it on the God behind the Scriptures, to see what He was doing. In this passage we can see that the invisible God, by the words of His Son, led people to consider their own sins, fulfilling His will. In verses 3–4, we read,

"And the scribes and Pharisees brought unto him a woman taken in adultery; and when they had set her in the midst,"

"They say unto him, Master, this woman was taken in adultery, in the very act."

A woman was caught committing adultery, and she was brought in the presence of Jesus. She was guilty as charged. But we will see what Jesus was led to do even though she was guilty. Verses 5–6 give us the words of the scribes and Pharisees who reminded Jesus of the law of Moses.

"Now Moses in the law commanded us, that such should be stoned: but what sayest thou [do you say]?"

"This they said, tempting him, that they might have to accuse him. But Jesus stooped down, and with his finger wrote on the ground, as though he heard them not."

In verse 5, it is given that in the law of Moses, in the Old Testament, under the old covenant, her punishment should have been stoning to death. The reference verse to this law is in Leviticus, chapter 20, verse 10, in which both the man and the woman were to be put to death. Under the old covenant, stones would have been gathered, and the judgment would have been executed. But the scribes and Pharisees were curious to know what Jesus would say concerning the situation with the woman and the sin. Jesus' response is in verse 7, and we'll look at verse 8, which says,

> "So when they continued asking him, he lifted up himself, and said unto them, He that is without sin among you, let him first cast a stone at her."

> "And again he stooped down, and wrote on the ground."

There doesn't seem to be an indication of what was written by Jesus, but it does mention the finger of Jesus. Being that God was in Jesus (2 Corinthians 5:19), God was there when that finger was writing. The other two places that mention something that had been written with God's finger are in Exodus chapter 31, verse 18, and Deuteronomy chapter 9, verse 10. In these we see that the two tablets of stone, having on them the Commandments of God, were given to Moses and were "written with the finger of God." That's just a thought though. But note that it is written in John, chapter 12, verses 49–50, that Jesus said,

> "For I have not spoken of myself; but the Father which sent me, he gave me a commandment, what I should say, and what I should speak."

> "Whatsoever I speak therefore, even as the Father said unto me, so I speak."

Looking at these two verses, it's clear that when Jesus spoke something, it was only what God had told Him to speak. He heard, or discerned, His Father's words and spoke them. It was the very word for word of God, through the mouth of His Son. So, when Jesus was in the presence of the Pharisees, scribes, and the woman who was caught in adultery, He spoke only what God gave Him to speak out.

Being that He didn't answer immediately when they asked Him what He had to say about it, most likely God had not given Him words yet. It's very likely He stooped the first time and wrote on the ground *while waiting on words from His Father*; words of wisdom, "like apples of gold in pictures of silver," which Proverbs, chapter 25, verse 11 describes. It's very likely that in that short moment of silence, God went in and searched all those hearts that surrounded the adulterous woman to see what sins were in them, and then the Word of the Lord came to Him, saying (v.7),

> "He that is without sin among you, let him first cast a stone at her."

In Jeremiah, chapter 17, verse 10, God said, "I the Lord search the heart." God has revealed that He searches, not searched or will search, but searches the hearts of people, in saying, "I...search." God goes throughout the earth, town by town, city by city, searching hearts.

Again, Jesus' answer, which He received from God, was, "He that is without sin among you, let him first cast a stone at her." The one without sin was the one who would be able to initiate the death sentence. All of them didn't have to be sin free, only one, and he could begin the throwing. The result was that not one of them cast a stone, therefore, each of them found sin within themselves. This is where we begin to see God dealing with people who judge others' sins, and know His will in the matter. Verse 9 tells us,

> "And they which heard it, being convicted by their own conscience, went out one by one, beginning at the eldest, even unto the last: and Jesus was left alone, and the woman standing in the midst."

When the men around the woman heard Jesus speak what He did, something began to happen. Initially, the scribes and the Pharisees were ready to get stones and cast them in the direction of their thoughts, at the evident sinner. Yet, at that moment, God gave Jesus words to speak that led them to turn their thoughts off the sin of another and onto their own sins. He led them into self-judgment. Their thoughts moved off the woman, off the other sinner, and onto themselves. As they each had their thoughts directed to their own guilt, we can see that their determination to carry out judgment on another ceased. They were convicted, as verse 9 says,

> "And they which heard it, being convicted by their own conscience, went out one by one."

Do you see what God the Father and Jesus the Son did that day? When they who heard it began to consider their own sins, the sins they were secretly walking around with, conviction came, and they were not as determined to destroy, judge, or kill the woman for her sin. It's possible that they had committed adultery in their hearts prior to that moment, because of the verses previously stated, "for wherein thou judgest another, thou condemnest thyself; for thou that judgest doest the same things." They were possibly guilty of the same, but it's not certain. It seems that when we who judge understand that our sins look just as bad on us as the sins of others look on them, that knowledge changes us. In the book of Malachi, chapter 3, verse 6, God said,

> "For I am the Lord, I change not."

What God accomplished with the scribes and Pharisees that day is what He wants to accomplish with us today. Today He tries to lead us to judge ourselves so that judgment won't have to come from Him. His judgment comes as a chastening, so that we won't be condemned with the rest of the world, as the apostle Paul said. So let us learn to "judge not," that we won't be judged.

Guess Who Will Judge the World?

Let's look at a bigger picture on the purpose of self-judgment. Those of us who are sealed by the Spirit of God, and have read the inspired Word of God, are aware of the Scriptures that speak of the day of judgment to come. We are familiar with the great white throne of God (Revelation

20:11) in front of which the dead will be judged by the books that will be opened. We read of the judgments to come on those who will refuse to repent in the years of the tribulation. It is made known throughout Scripture that God is the "Judge of all the earth" (Genesis 18:25). He is a Judge, who judges. The redeemed are the children of that Judge, and He has given them instructions about who and how they are to learn to judge in this life, for a greater purpose.

Consider these verses in 1 Corinthians, in which the apostle Paul made some very enlightening statements about the saints and judgment. Paul wrote of this subject to the believers in his days, who lacked the ability to judge their matters among themselves. They apparently had gone to the unbelievers in law to judge their matters. Paul then informed them of this, in 1 Corinthians, chapter 6, verse 2:

> "Do ye not know that the saints shall judge the world?
> and if the world shall be judged by you, are ye unworthy
> to judge the smallest matters?"

Notice who he said will judge the world. "The saints shall judge the world." In the book of Matthew, chapter 7, verses 22–23, it reveals that Jesus is the One to announce who will or won't get into the kingdom of heaven, but the saints will be involved in judging the world. This is what the apostle Paul said, and he received his revelation from Jesus. The word *judged* in the second line of this verse means to try and condemn. The word *saints* means the holy ones, those to whom Paul wrote the letter. They are labeled as "the church of God," and those "sanctified in Christ Jesus" (1 Corinthians 1:2). The saints are not whom man deems to be saints, but those whom God Himself has called and sanctified. In verse 3, Paul went on to say,

> "Know ye not that we shall judge angels?"

Paul made it clear that the redeemed are also to judge the angels, most likely the fallen angels (see 2 Peter 2:4). The world and the angels are to be judged by saints. If the saints, who are the redeemed, are to be involved in the judgment of the world, then the process of growing in God's knowledge, learning to judge matters in life righteously (as the Holy Spirit teaches), and judging ourselves, as Scripture tells us to, will serve a much greater purpose that is yet to come.

The redeemed are to learn God's righteousness, because there is a righteous kingdom coming to earth, in which Jesus will rule as King. The Lord is establishing His kingdom on earth, and we are basically in training to serve in that coming kingdom. So, if all this judging is to take place and the redeemed are to do some judging, where do the redeemed begin?

Well, the Scriptures address the topic of judging, along with how and whom we are to begin judging. It may come as a surprise to many children of the Judge, but we are not called to judge the world now. However, we are instructed to do some judging, which is called self-judging. We start with us and prepare for what's soon to come. It's important that we learn this, and we'll look at some other verses to find out why.

Judgment Has Begun

There is yet another bigger picture to look at concerning judgment, us, and God. As mentioned previously, the children of God know of the coming day of judgment, when the books will be opened for judgment. But here is something enlightening to think about. Consider what is given in 1 Peter, chapter 4, verse 17, about judgment:

> "For the time is come that judgment must begin at the house of God: and if it first begin at us, what shall the end be of them that obey not the gospel of God?"

When you collect an abundance of facts on any subject, you get a greater understanding about that subject. Viewing all these verses with their details tends to bring us into a much better focus about the subject of judgment. Let's first focus on these words:

> "For the time is come that judgment must begin."

This is a very interesting fact to realize. Peter proclaimed that in his days the time had come, "that judgment must begin." Well, has judgment begun? Could it be that judgment is taking place, now? According to Peter, who was inspired by the Holy Spirit, judgment has already begun. But where has it started? Peter said judgment had to begin,

"at the house of God."

Basically, we can say that at God's house is His family. Correct? God's family members are—being judged first. We are apparently in judgment as of right now. Since the days that salvation came, those who are accepting Jesus and moving into God's family are the first to be judged, tried in the refiner's fire, chastened, corrected, and refined for the kingdom of righteousness to come.

This is why Jesus and Paul taught that we should learn to judge ourselves, or God will have to judge us. The reason is that judgment has begun, and it's begun with us. If we let the Holy Spirit teach us to discern our own sins, learn why we do them, learn of the damage it causes in life, learn how correct ourselves and repent, and all else involved, we are letting Him teach us things about judgment. By the time we go through the process of fixing ourselves by the leading of the Holy Spirit, and judging other matters in righteousness, we will have learned much about judgment.

While the world will be condemned, the redeemed will have been refined. Paul wrote that "we shall all stand before the judgment seat of Christ" (Romans 14:10) and give an account of ourselves. But the redeemed who have repented won't have to stand at the judgment seat under condemnation, along with those who will be judged and condemned by the books that will be opened and used at that time. Now that judgment has begun, God is using the "books" of the Bible to teach and correct those in "the house of God" (2 Timothy 3:16).

Can you see that judgment has already begun? Do you perceive what God is doing? Therefore, it's best that we learn to stop judging others and get serious about judging ourselves instead. It's educational, and it's preparation. It's time for us to understand what God is doing and get prepared. In Jesus' words in Matthew, chapter 7, verses 21–23,

He makes it clear how serious it is that we learn to evaluate ourselves and repent, or else. He said,

> "Not everyone that saith unto me, Lord, Lord, shall enter into the kingdom of heaven; but he that doeth the will of my Father which is in heaven."

> "Many will say to me in that day, Lord, Lord, have we not prophesied in thy [your] name? and in thy name have cast out devils? and in thy name done many wonderful works?"

> "And then will I profess unto them, I never knew you: depart from me, ye that work iniquity."

On the day of judgment, at the last moment, at the last second, "many" who had known to call Jesus Lord will hear Him say, "Depart from me," not "Welcome." Notice the reason why. The deciding factor will not be the gift of prophesying in His name, nor miracle working in His name. He stated that those who "work iniquity" will not be welcomed. To work iniquity means to practice lawlessness, or sin. Calling Jesus Lord won't grant a pardon on that day, according to this verse, but turning from iniquity shows here to be the deciding factor. Stopping the sin habit, or practicing repentance. Didn't Jesus tell His followers to preach repentance (Luke 24:47)?

God is seriously trying to fix us, so let's submit and let Him. When those who have refused Jesus stand in judgment, they will be condemned having lived lawless lives. And remember who will be judging the world—the saints. We better heed these instructions and follow the Holy Spirit out of iniquity, learn to judge ourselves, and repent. Truly the kingdom of heaven is near.

If you do not practice evaluating yourself and would like to begin taking your focus off others' issues, take your request to God. Scripture tells us, "Ask, and it shall be given you" (Matthew 7:7). Following is a prayer to God for a new direction in the matter of judging, if you feel the need to do so. He will hear your words. God bless you in your walk with Him.

Prayer

Lord, thank You for sending your Son Jesus, who died on the
cross for my sins and made a way that I can come to You
behind the veil. Your Word says that if I need wisdom, I can ask
You for it. Lord, I understand that You do not want me to
judge other people. Will You give me wisdom to understand if I am
judging others and to learn not to do so, but rather to judge
myself and discern when I am doing wrong? Your Word says that
if we ask anything according to Your will, You hear us
and will grant it to us. I thank You for hearing me today
in this request. In Jesus' name I pray, amen.

Chapter 7

Jesus Brings Freedom to Tormented Souls

This chapter is a study of a tormented soul that is written of in the books of Matthew, Mark, and Luke. Scriptures taken from the Gospels of Luke and Mark are used in this study to compare what is given on this subject. Luke's account is in chapter 8, verses 26–40, and Mark's account is in chapter 5, verses 1–20. This is a deep spiritual look into the effect of the Enemy on humanity, the powerful impact that Jesus has in one's life, and the glorious freedom from the kingdom of darkness that Jesus offers to each of us. This study offers a glimpse of the effects of both the kingdom of darkness, and the kingdom of light on humanity. The man mentioned in these verses had a legion of evil spirits within him. He was in need of miraculous help, and that he received. Romans, chapter 15, verse 4, tells us,

> "For whatsoever things were written aforetime [previously] were written for our learning."

These Scriptures are here for us to learn from. Answers to life are found in these writings. God freely gives us His knowledge, because it's His will for us to have this wisdom. If it's in the Bible, it's for us to learn. I think it's amazing that the same God who created the heavens and the earth by His knowledge wants to share His knowledge with us. All we have to do is ask Him for it, receive it when He gives it, and apply it.

This study draws much attention to the details about the spiritual and physical state of a man with many evil spirits, to help understand some things about the spiritual side of our battles. What is also revealed is the power Jesus has over all evil spirits. As in any war, the more details you know about your enemy, the more prepared you are for the battle, and a victory.

Where Did Evil Spirits Come From?

Let's briefly look at some verses on the origin of God's unseen enemies, where they came from, and what they do. Let's first look at some verses that give knowledge about the two unseen spiritual kingdoms, and their battle for souls. In reading Ephesians, chapter 6, verse 12, we learn where our battles and struggles actually come from:

> "For we wrestle not against flesh and blood, but against principalities, against powers, against the rulers of the darkness of this world, against spiritual wickedness in high places."

Notice the word "wrestle" in this verse. Other terms for this are *struggle, battle, fighting,* or even *warring.* Consider how many times we hear of someone battling something in life, fighting an issue in life, or struggling with something in life, such as an addiction. There are many struggles we encounter in life, and Scripture reveals they are not against "flesh and blood." Flesh and blood are in the physical realm, but the struggles and battles we encounter involve the spiritual realm. "Rulers of the darkness" and "spiritual wickedness," though unseen, are the source or our battles. Something unseen is on the move attacking God's creation. Always be aware of this fact.

Evil spirits, enemies of God, are out to destroy God's creation, especially targeting those who keep God's Commandments (see Revelation 12:17). In Revelation, chapter 9, verse 11, it gives the names of the king of the spirits that come out the pit of the earth that bring destruction with them. In Greek his name is Apollyon, which means Destroyer. The Hebrew name is Abaddon. He is the angel of the bottomless pit, according to John's vision. The apostle Paul revealed that this is the source of our battles, saying we *wrestle* with them. The battles are spiritual. Revelation, chapter 12, verses 7–9 explain an interesting fact about where the Devil and his demons came from.

> "And there was war in heaven: Michael and his angels fought against the dragon; and the dragon fought and his angels,"

> "And prevailed not; neither was their place found anymore in heaven."

> "And the great dragon was cast out, that old serpent, called the Devil, and Satan, which deceiveth [deceives] the whole world: he was cast out into the earth, and his angels were cast out with him."

"There was war in heaven." Of all the wars in history that we are able to read of today, the most important one to know of is the one that took place in heaven. Michael the archangel, and his holy angels, battled "the dragon," who is Satan, and "his angels." Michael is written of in the book of Daniel as a chief prince. He is one who has great authority in God's kingdom. We see this in reading that he fought with "his angels." Please note that Satan also has angels. Satan was high in rank (Ezekiel 28:13–15) and had many angels under his authority. They followed Satan in his rebellion, and the result of that rebellion is written of in verse 9, which states,

> "He was cast out into the earth, and his angels were cast out with him."

The Devil came from heaven, along with the angels (demons) that rebelled with him. Satan was an anointed cherub who turned against God, became His Enemy, divided His army, and was thrown out of God's kingdom of heaven, along with the angels that were under his authority. Jesus said that a kingdom divided will not stand (Mark 3:24), therefore God threw Satan and those under him out of His kingdom. We can learn something very, very important here about the effect leaders have on those they lead; the angels under Satan turned against

God with him. It is revealed in Scripture (Revelation 12:4) that one third of the angels turned against God and righteousness, with Satan as their leader. As you read of Job, Satan also tried to turn Job against God, but failed.

Another fact to know and understand is that they are spirits of darkness because they no longer have access to God's glory light, which they once took part of in His presence, being His angels. It is written in Scripture that Moses went in the presence of God, and his face shone so very bright after leaving God's presence that he had to veil his face. Since the wicked angels have been thrown out of God's presence, they lack the glory light and cannot emit it. Therefore, they are shadowed and dark spirits.

The rebellious part of the host were cast out of heaven, will never return, and eternal torment in the lake of fire has been their chosen destiny. What most people don't know is that these wicked angels have been thrown down to the earth. When they were thrown out of heaven and down to earth, verse 10 reveals that it was then proclaimed in the vision, "Now is come salvation." Salvation came when Jesus came. Jesus apparently saw a vision of Satan being cast out of heaven, because in Luke, chapter 10, verse 18, it's written that Jesus said,

"I beheld Satan as lightning fall from heaven."

God revealed to His Son that Satan had fallen, and that he was thrown out. Before the days that the Messiah had come, it was revealed to Isaiah that Satan was to be thrown out of heaven. He wrote of it in Isaiah, chapter 14, verse 12, saying,

"How art thou fallen from heaven, O Lucifer, son of the morning!"

When Satan was cast out, Jesus was to go to the cross as the Lamb of God to take the punishment for our sins. Satan and his angels were cast down from heaven, and Jesus was going up having all authority in heaven and earth given to Him (see Matthew 28:18).

Satan and his fallen angels make up the kingdom of darkness (Acts 26:18), which takes people captive. For example, in 2 Timothy, chapter 2, verse 26, we read that people "are taken captive by him." Luke, chapter 13, verse 16, tells of a woman "whom Satan hath bound." In 1 Timothy chapter 3, verse 7, it mentions "the snare of the devil." These are war scene terms. These are terms used in Scripture to describe what the Devil and his kingdom of darkness do. They snare, tie up, and take captive God's creation, like the enemies do in war movies on television. The spiritual realm is the same, yet it's done spiritually. We become tied up spiritually, and possibly tormented as a prisoner of war. This we'll look into concerning the man with the legion of demons. Scripture actually reveals what being tied up spiritually looks like. It is seen in society everyday, yet it's not understood.

Jesus, the King of Kings, came "to preach deliverance to the captives," and set them free. This He proclaimed (Luke 4:18). He came preaching deliverance and freedom to those snared by the Devil. Jesus is a King who offers us spiritual freedom.

Jesus Is Sent to the Captives

A very good example of the freedom Jesus can bring us is found in the case of the man who had a legion of Satan's host within him. In Mark, chapter 4, verse 35, Jesus told His disciples they were to go over to the other side of the Sea of Galilee. Jesus made it clear that He did nothing other than what the Father showed Him to do. John, chapter 5, verse 19, says of Jesus,

> "Verily, verily, I say unto you, The Son can do nothing of himself, but what he seeth [sees] the Father do: for what things soever he doeth [does], these also doeth [does] the Son likewise."

Jesus explained that He only did "what he seeth the Father do." Jesus saw God deliver the tormented man from the hand of Satan. He most likely a saw a vision from God. God sent Jesus intentionally to that man, at that time. What the man didn't know was that God saw him and his need, and help was on the way. Miraculous freedom was coming to a man in the country of the Gad-a-renes'. Mark, chapter 5, verses 1–3, reads,

> "And they came over unto the other side of the sea, into the country of the Gad-a-renes'."

> "And when he was come out of the ship, immediately there met him out of the tombs a man with an unclean spirit."

> "Who had his dwelling among the tombs; and no man could bind him, no, not with chains."

In verse 2 it tells us that when Jesus arrived at Gad-a-renes', "there met him out of the tombs a man with an unclean spirit." This man came to Jesus from the tombs, and the writer plainly states what his issue was in saying he had "an unclean spirit." Something unseen was affecting this man's life. This information helps us understand the mysteries concerning many problems we have in life.

Now we will move from Mark's account to Luke's, to see what Luke was divinely inspired to write about him. In Luke, chapter 8, verse 27, it says this about Jesus coming in contact with the man:

> "And when he went forth to land, there met him out of the city a certain man, which had devils longtime, and ware [wore] no clothes, neither abode in any house, but in the tombs."

Luke said this man had "devils [a] long time." Matthew said the man had "an unclean spirit." A demon (devil) is an unclean spirit. They are referred to as unclean, because they are filthy in their words and ways in the eyes of God. Having demons, he stayed among tombs.

In Ephesians chapter 6, verse 12, as previously mentioned, it tells us that we are also wrestling, or battling, with spiritual wickedness, or unclean spirits. It wasn't only his problem then; the same spirits are roaming earth today. They don't die, they keep roaming, and will until they're cast into the eternal fire. Jesus informed us in John, chapter 15, verse 5, "Without me ye can do nothing." Jesus turned this man's captivity, or rather loosed him from being a captive. Freedom from captivity comes only from Jesus and what He has done for us on the cross. Captivity does need to be better understood and recognized for what it is.

I recall being bound in alcoholism, and it wasn't until I verbally surrendered my life to Jesus that the shackles of the addiction fell off. I didn't know at the time that I'd been taken captive by a spirit of addiction. The reason I wasn't able to quit the addiction was because I became bound in it. I was trapped in my sin, and needed help. I walked right into the trap, as so many others have done throughout the generations. I wasn't enlightened to the truth of the matter until the Holy Spirit revealed it to me, after being baptized by the Holy Spirit.

Without Jesus being Lord of our lives, we can't understand why we can't get out of the fornication, drunkenness, addictions, fears, pride, self-hatred, hatred of others, anger, and so forth. But the reality is that each of these is a sin, and when we engage in them, that is the bait Satan and his demons use to ensnare us. We then become held as captives in these sins by an unseen enemy. When we can't stop bad habits, it's because we have become bound, or held, in them. The way out is confession of the sin, and repentance. But if a person does not know what sin is, the sin can't be confessed, and repentance is not likely to happen. Therefore, freedom won't come. Jesus is the One who educates us about these things, and leads us to freedom.

I recall very clearly, after being born into God's family, when I realized that God did not want me to smoke cigarettes anymore. Promptings came from God about this, and one day I decided to stop smoking. Well, when you decide to stop sinning, beware—the host of hell will show up to battle you in your mind to hold you in the sin. Many may wonder why it is so difficult to stop smoking. The answer is that the smoker is a victim of Satan's snare. Smoking is a sin, and the smoker becomes bound in the sin. The struggle to stop is the struggle to be released from captivity.

Several years ago I was in my kitchen reading in my Bible at midday. It was either the day I quite, or the day after, when the attacks in my mind intensified, and I was getting irritated. The thoughts had been with me for about fifteen years, but that day they were annoying me. Previously God had given me the spiritual gift of discerning of spirits (1 Corinthians 12:10), but I was not yet educated in the ability to discern. That battle was perhaps the first Jesus used to teach me about discerning the unseen Enemy, and how to do battle in the unseen realm.

On that particular day my thoughts were harassed with "Smoke a cigarette," "Just one more cigarette," "Quit tomorrow," or "Smoke just half a cigarette." These harassing thoughts came over, and over, and over again, and I was getting agitated by them. I couldn't read the Bible because of those annoying thoughts. This is what demons do to get you to give in and keep sinning, they harass. What I didn't immediately know was that these thoughts were from an unseen, fallen angel that was cast out of heaven (Revelation 12:9).

What I did next was began to speak back out loud in a low tone to the irritating thoughts, "No, I don't smoke!" "I said I don't smoke!" "No, I'm not doing it." What was taking place was a battle, though I didn't know it yet. I began to battle spiritual wickedness (Ephesians 6:12) and close a door in my life that had been opened to the demonic earlier in my life. I had ignorantly given them place in me to sin against God and hold me captive, but they were then being kicked out with force.

Whenever we give in to the thoughts of sin, we give the enemy an open door to take us captive, and he will. Part of our battle is casting such thoughts out. In 2 Corinthians, chapter 10, verse 5, we are told to get rid of the thoughts that are contrary to the Word of God. Well, the thought of putting smoke in my lungs is contrary to the Word of God. The thought to smoke was being cast out.

In the midst of speaking out words such as "No, I'm not going to smoke!" with a hint of an angry tone, the Holy Spirit—then showed up—to help, and something happened within my spirit. Praise God! He had seen and heard my battle cry to repent, and He sent words of knowledge. Revelation knowledge came at that very moment to help me with my battle. I now realize He showed up to reveal truth, which in turn advanced me to freedom from being bound in that sin. Hebrews, chapter 4, verse 12, states,

> "For the word of God is quick, and powerful, and sharper than any twoedged sword, piercing even to the dividing asunder of soul and spirit."

Very clear thoughts such as, "I was not born to be a smoker," "I was truly not a smoker," and "I truly didn't want to smoke," began to surface. Revealed truth began to move in and pierce as a "twoedged sword," which divided asunder (separated) this lying spirit from myself. I thought I wanted to smoke, but when this invisible enemy of righteousness departed from me, and I perceived when he did, my thoughts then became miraculously clear about the truth. I then realized who was standing next to me saying, "Smoke another cigarette."

I began to realize what was happening. He was being detected and that's what he doesn't want. I was basically looking at someone I could not see, and exchanging words in the battle with whom I could not see. But God revealed to me, "He's there." Jesus did this when He was tempted in the wilderness, did he not? He heard the words, detected the Enemy, and fought back with His words of truth, saying, "It is written".

When knowledge came from the Holy Spirit, the battle turned in my favor. I began to discern the Enemy—where he was, what he was doing to me—and then I had an aim. I fired back. I became bold! I said out loud, "I said I don't smoke! Go somewhere else and sin, because you won't be sinning through me anymore. Get out of here in Jesus' name!"

The battle didn't last long, and I never smoked again. I haven't had a desire to smoke since then, because that desire had come from an evil spirit. When he left, the desire left, and the harassing thoughts to smoke left also. God showed me it was the unclean spirit's desire, not mine. What I did in ignorance was give them an open door to come in and defile me.

Here's a fact. Smokers may think they like to smoke, but they were not born with that desire. Sometime in life, the person took part in the sin and unknowingly allowed in an evil, unclean spirit with its strong desire. The spirit is not detected, but the desire to smoke starts to manifest all the time. Both are then sinning in the eyes of God. Unclean spirits desire to sin, and they want to sin through our vessels, our bodies. When we engage in sin we give them access, and then we become defiled before God.

I now think of it in this way. It is written that the body of the believer is the New Covenant temple of God. Well, Old Testament Scripture reveals that God struck down those who had burned strange incense before Him when He said not to (Leviticus 10:1). To smoke is like burning strange incense in the temple (the body) before the Lord. It literally stinks up the temple.

I had given the Enemy an open door to my life to use me in sin, in the eyes of God. I took control by battling the thoughts with boldness, after the Holy Spirit revealed truth to me at that moment. As Jesus said, "Ye shall know the truth, and the truth shall make you free" (John 8:32). It did. I then knew which thoughts were not mine. You may not realize this, but many thoughts that surface within are not your own. That's why Jesus said cast them out, but first they need to be discerned. Thoughts need to be sifted like wheat in biblical times; the bad stuff needs to be blown away.

Revealed truth opens the door to freedom. Jesus offers this to us. "The word of God is quick [living], and powerful, and sharper than any twoedged sword...and is a discerner of the thoughts and intents of the heart" (Hebrews 4:12). Studying what is written in the Bible helps us discern which thoughts aren't godly thoughts, which thoughts need to be removed, and which thoughts to replace them with.

The Captive's Condition

Let's look at the condition of the man who lived among the tombs. There are several distinguishing traits to note about him that are identified with demonic oppression. Back in the Gospel of Mark, chapter 5, verses 3–4, it tells us of the man:

"Who had his dwelling among the tombs; and no man could bind him, no, not with chains:"

"Because that he had been often bound with fetters and chains, and the chains had been plucked asunder by him, and the fetters broken in pieces: neither could any man tame him."

The word *fetters* used here means shackles. In Luke's account we read that this man had devils, and here in Mark's account we find some traits of a person having the influence of demons (devils). For example, verse 3 tells us,

"No man could bind him, no, not with chains."

There had apparently been attempts to restrain him with chains and were unsuccessful, at least at keeping him chained, because verse 4 says, "the chains had been plucked asunder by him." The man with demons had supernatural strength. Someone influenced by a demon can have strength beyond normal. Verse 4 then says,

"Neither could any man tame him."

The man with demons was untamable. If he needed to be tamed, then we can know that he was wild. Wild means uncontrolled, causing violence or disturbance, erratic, uncivilized, and unruly. So according to scripture, demons will drive a person to be wild, while God brings peaceable calmness to the soul and mind. In Matthew's account he referred to the man (men) as "exceeding fierce." In Mark, chapter 5, verse 5, it gives us an understanding of the torment and spiritual state the man was in due to the oppression.

"And always, night and day, he was in the mountains, and in the tombs, crying, and cutting himself with stones."

This man had been driven away from people and family and was living a secluded life in the mountains, in what we would call the graveyard. (Please note that in Matthew's account, for some reason, there is mention of two men possessed with devils.)

Having the Devil's influence in his mind caused him to live among the dead. He wasn't mentally normal. Evil spirits altered his thoughts. That's what they do. The Word of God says that "Satan...deceiveth the whole world" (see Revelation 12:9). We who have been baptized by the Holy Spirit are required to renew our thinking (Romans 12:2) so that we can recognize it, and come out of that deception. We need our thoughts to be in unity with Jesus, who is truth. The man spoken of in these verses was in very bad shape. While in the graveyard he was,

"crying, and cutting himself with stones."

Today, a person behaving in this way would be diagnosed with psychological disorders. Today, he would be referred to as a "cutter." The Bible reveals that it's demons within the person. He would cut himself, bringing harm and pain to the body. The fact that he was crying while cutting indicates a state of mental torment. He was in a losing battle, until Jesus showed up in his life.

Demons are God's enemies who were thrown out of heaven, and this shows us what they are all about: self-destruction, hurting, and hating humanity. An enemy is someone who attacks or tries to harm you. This was and is the war with "spiritual wickedness" (Ephesians 6:12). It's as real today as it was in the days of Jesus. We all have battles in life, but if we know God's truth and are "doers of the word" (see James 1:22), doors to sin can be closed in our lives, which will deny the enemy entrance. Knowing what is in the Bible helps to understand the battles.

According to what has been looked at so far, here are some traits of the man influenced by demons:

- he wore no clothes (exposure of the body)
- he had strength beyond normal
- he lived secluded
- he lived among tombs

- he was wild in nature (could not be tamed)
- he was very fierce
- he cut on himself
- he cried and cried

The Devil leads people to live completely opposite of God's will. Luke wrote that he had many demons in him. The Scriptures refer to the amount as a legion, which will be observed in verses 9 and 13. Remember, Romans, chapter 15, verse 4 says, "For whatsoever things were written aforetime [previously] were written for our learning." These Scriptures are here to teach us about these mysteries of life, and God wants us to be knowledgeable of these things. In 2 Timothy, chapter 3, verse 16, it is written that, "All scripture is given by inspiration of God." This includes all information about Satan and his demons. It's God ordained.

In the next several verses, watch how this situation unfolded when the Savior of the world showed up in his presence. God had sent Jesus to that man on that day, and oh what a glorious day it was for that tormented soul, hallelujah! Jesus is our hope. Mark, chapter 5, verses 6-8, tell us,

> "But when he saw Jesus afar off, he ran and worshipped him."

> "And cried with a loud voice, and said, What have I to do with thee [you], Jesus, thou Son of the most high God? I adjure thee by God, that thou torment me not."

> "For he said unto him, Come out of the man, thou [you] unclean spirit."

When Jesus showed up, He knew what the man's problem was. He said, "Come out of the man, thou unclean spirit." Jesus addressed the man's spiritual issues. He commanded the evil spirit to come out. There was an attempt to chain him because he was obviously a threat to himself and others, yet he was already bound up by demons. He was bound for a long time in a destructive mental state. The Bible refers to this man's condition as being bound by Satan (see Luke 13:16). He was stuck in his ways, mentally and physically, and tormented while being bound.

Jesus Set A Captive Free

We will now shift our attention to the glorious Son of God, and the possibilities that arise when He shows up in our lives. Hopefully your faith will be boosted when you think about these things, and know there is hope that lives can be changed even when there seems to be no hope. Proverbs, chapter 13, verse 12, enlightens us to this fact, "Hope deferred maketh [makes] the heart sick." How awful it is when life's circumstances become overwhelming and there seems to be nothing that offers much hope. But Jesus came offering us an abundance of hope, concerning everything. Let's consider the hope we have in Him, as we read about this man's deliverance from the kingdom of darkness. Verses 8 and 9 read,

> "For he said unto him, Come out of the man, thou unclean spirit."

> "And he asked him, What is thy name? And he answered, saying, My name is Legion: for we are many."

Notice the answer given from the man: "My name is Legion: for we are many." Why would one man say, "we are many"? That doesn't make sense. What does make sense is that it wasn't the man speaking, but the demons in him. The demons spoke through the man to the Son of God.

Spirits of darkness that have been cast out of heaven, down to the earth, speak out of the mouths of people. This may sound strange, but it's only because this knowledge is not known and taught. Jesus had rebuked the Devil speaking through the mouth of Peter, His follower, just before going to the cross to die for our sins (see Peter 16:22–23). But, Scripture does reveal that the Holy Spirit also speaks out through those who surrender their lives to Him (Matthew 10:20).

In the statement, "My name is Legion: for we are many," the word *legion* means a body of soldiers, or a large multitude. It was a portion of the host of Satan. Verse 13 reveals more about this, but let's now look into verses 10–12, which state,

> "And he besought him much that he would not send them away out of the country."

> "Now there was there nigh unto the mountains a great herd of swine feeding."

> "And all the devils besought him, saying, Send us into the swine, that we may enter into them."

Here we have a confrontation between Jesus and a multitude of unclean spirits. Mark's account offers us something very interesting, which is in verse 10, saying,

> "And he besought him much that he would not send them away out of the country."

For some reason the demons didn't want to be sent "out of the country," which apparently Jesus could have done. There are a few things we can see in Scripture about what Jesus commanded evil spirits when they were cast out of someone. In Mark, chapter 9, verse 25, Jesus commanded a spirit to come out a man's son and ordered the spirit *not to return*. In Mark, chapter 1, verse 25, there was a command given *only to come out* of a man. Here in Mark's account, we find that the demons were very much aware that they might have had to *leave the country* at the command of Jesus. But in Luke's account, chapter 8, verse 31, the demons' request is stated a little differently. He wrote:

> "And they besought him that he would not command them to go out into the deep."

In this verse the word "deep" is translated in the New International Version as the abyss, the lower regions of the earth where hell is presently located. So the demons were begging Jesus not to send them out of the country, or down to hell. What this tells us is that they knew the power (authority) of Jesus, and wherever Jesus told them to go, they had to go, even if it was down to the torments of hell. I point this out because back in Mark, chapter 5, verses 6–7, it states the words that the demons spoke out to Jesus when He showed up in the area. What they said was,

"But when he saw Jesus afar off, he ran and worshipped him,"

"And cried with a loud voice, and said, What have I to do with thee, Jesus, thou Son of the most high God? I adjure thee by God, that thou torment me not."

There is something that should be exposed about demons here in these verses. The demons were pleading with Jesus to *not torment them*, which Jesus could have ordered. We know it was not the man saying "torment me not," because it makes no sense that Jesus would torment him. It was the words of the demons. They knew there was a possibility of them being sent to hell, where there is torment. But notice their request:

"I adjure thee by God, that thou torment me not."

The Holy Spirit drew my attention to this bit of information. Those demons pleaded with the powerful Son of God to not torment them, or send them where they would be tormented. Yet, what were they guilty of doing? Tormenting a man, for a long time—how wicked! There they were, pleading with Jesus to not be tormented like they had been doing to someone else.

This brought my thoughts back to Cain and Abel in Genesis, chapter 4, verses 8–14. After Cain killed Abel, his brother, God's judgment fell upon him. He then complained about the judgment being more than he could bear and was concerned that someone would find him and kill him. He had killed his brother, yet he didn't want to be killed. That's the mind of the Devil. He doesn't want done to him what he does to others.

But what is the mind of God? In Matthew, chapter 7, verse 12, Jesus said, "All things whatsoever ye would that men should do to you, do ye even so to them." Treat others as you would like to be treated, says God, yet wicked spirits treat others as they don't want to be treated themselves. So, what did Jesus do with the request of the evil spirits? In Mark chapter 5, verse 12, this is what they requested from Jesus:

"Send us into the swine."

They could no longer stay in the man, and they certainly did not want to go to hell. The evil spirits knew they had to move out at Jesus' command. They knew then, as they do now, that Jesus has authority over all of them in Satan's kingdom. And their desire was to go where? Into the pigs. Knowing the pigs were nearby, the demons requested to go there. They had to go wherever Jesus was to send them, and He allowed them to go into the pigs.

Here's an interesting thought. As wicked as the demons were, they had their request granted. They were able to go into the pigs. Why would we think Jesus won't give us our desires in the process of following Him? Those demons didn't get tormented in the abyss prematurely that day. That's just something to think about. What might it look like when demons enter pigs? Mark, chapter 5, verse 13, states,

> "And forth with Jesus gave them leave [permission].
> And the unclean spirits went out, and entered into the
> swine: and the herd ran violently down a steep place
> into the sea, (they were about two thousand;) and were
> choked in the sea."

Notice what took place when the evil spirits entered into the pigs: "the herd ran violently." Here we see a trace of the kingdom of darkness: being violent. The spirits were not seen, but the evidence of their presence was that the pigs' behavior suddenly became violent. Violent behavior comes from demons. Where did they run to? They headed to the water, in which they drowned. Self-destruction entered the minds when the evil spirits moved in.

The minds of both the man and the pigs were altered by the influence of demons. The man was driven to harm himself (self-destruction), and the pigs drowned themselves (self-destruction). So demons alter the thoughts in a destructive way. Being mentally unstable is a result of evil spirits being present, according to God's Word.

Earlier, in verse 9, it was written that the name of the demon was "Legion," because there were many in the man. Verse 13 tells us that about 2000 pigs ran violently into the water. This means there were about 2,000 demons that bothered this man, and they all left when Jesus said, "Go!" Wow! That's our Savior! That's our Jesus! That's the Son of God! That is the King of Kings, amen!

What Freedom Looks Like

Let's now read about the blessing that came to the tormented soul that day. What happened to this man when Jesus showed up in his life is a great illustration of what freedom in Christ is like. There are a few things to consider about how his freedom came and the effect it had on his life, which I want to point out.

God saw the need and sent His Son. Jesus showed up in his life first. Then, in the presence of Jesus he became delivered, and liberated. After the awesome liberation, he desired greatly to follow Jesus.

Likewise, God saw our need and sent Jesus to die on the cross for the penalty for our sins. It is not until we accept Jesus into our life that we become liberated. When we accept Jesus into our hearts, He resides within us and we are then always in His presence. We then become liberated, as Jesus drives out the evil from within us. From this amazing, life-changing experience that takes place within, we desire greatly to follow Jesus.

Just because we are not in the exact shape this man was in does not mean we don't need freedom in many areas in our lives, because we do. We all have sinned, Scripture says. Verses 14–15 of Mark, chapter 5, then reads,

> "And they that fed the swine fled, and told it in the city, and in the country. And they went out to see what it was that was done."

> "And they come to Jesus, and see him that was possessed with the devil, and had the legion, sitting, and clothed, and in his right mind: and they were afraid."

In these verses, we see a miracle had taken place in the life of a man who had been tormented by demons for a long time. How long? We don't know, but it was a long period of his life that was spent in misery. Just as we do today, the people who saw it went and told a bunch of other people. When others came to see what was going on, according to what was told to them, verse 15 tells us they saw the formerly possessed man,

> "sitting, and clothed, and in his right mind: and they were afraid."

Under the Devil's influence, he would not keep his clothes on, but Jesus set him free. For a long time, he had been cutting himself, but Jesus set him free. For a long time, he had been crying in misery, but Jesus set him free. For a long time, he had been mentally disturbed, but Jesus set him free. The Lord restored him to what is normal in the eyes of God—no more cutting, exposing himself, and living in misery and solitude. Demons are behind that behavior, not God.

From this we can see that Jesus came to clear up both our thinking and our actions. This results in freedom that is both felt within, and seen on the outside. Jesus can restore us to having a right mind. We act according to how we think (Proverbs 23:7), and Jesus brings us to a good righteous mental state, if we will allow Him to. Verse 18 then reads,

> "And when he [Jesus] was come into the ship, he that had been possessed with the devil prayed him that he might be with him."

The healed man wanted badly to go with Jesus, who had set him free and made him feel better, but that was not in Jesus' plans. This actually shows the truth of how Jesus draws people to Him by what He offers. When Jesus impacts a person's life by the power He demonstrates, when He manifests, that impact draws the person to Him. For those who have not experienced the impact of the saving power of Jesus in their life, they have no clue as to what He offers, both now and for eternity. It's called salvation.

The life of the man in torment was impacted by the power of Jesus, and what he experienced on the inside led him to beg Jesus to let him go wherever Jesus was going. Jesus worked a miracle inside the man, and it showed on the outside. This is how He works. We invite Him to come into our hearts and some miraculous, powerful things began to happen within. This powerful experience is so overwhelmingly desirable, we are then drawn daily to this inner effect from Him. The touch of Jesus is very desirable. Verse 19 then reads,

> "Howbeit Jesus suffered him not, but saith [said] unto him, Go home to thy friends, and tell them how great things the Lord hath [has] done for thee [thee], and hath had compassion on thee."

Jesus "had compassion" on the man in his condition, and had relieved him of the hold that the kingdom of darkness had on him. He had been taken captive; he had been bound by Satan, but the King of Glory showed up and gave him what He gives, freedom. Verse 20 states,

> "And he departed, and began to publish in De-cap'-o-lis how great things Jesus had done for him: and all men did marvel."

What a great day it was for that man to go home healed and in his right mind, looking forward to a normal life again. Hallelujah! What a testimony he had. He went to the city, not back to the tombs. God had given him freedom, and a new life. This man went home a believer in Jesus, the Son of God, because of the miracle of deliverance. We can all have new life when we invite the Holy Spirit to come into our hearts and let Him begin the process of deliverance with its powerful impact.

Jesus set him free that day, and this is what Jesus Messiah came to do for us. This is an example of His mercy, compassion, and power. Satan's kingdom is total wickedness, and God is calling people out of that kingdom of darkness, deception, and bondage, into His kingdom of truth and freedom. In Acts, chapter 26, verses 16–18, Jesus told the apostle Paul,

> "But rise, and stand upon thy feet: for I have appeared unto thee for this purpose, to make thee a minister and a witness both of these things which thou hast seen, and of those things in the which I will appear unto thee."

> "Delivering thee from the people, and from the Gentiles, unto whom now I send thee,"

> "To open their eyes, and to turn them from darkness to light, and from the power of Satan unto God, that they may receive forgiveness of sins."

The Lord revealed to Paul what he was called to do. He was sent to the Gentiles (non-Jews), "To open their eyes, and to turn them from... the power of Satan unto God." That's what God is trying to do. He is trying to turn people from Satan to Him. He wants to release people from Satan's hold, and to set them free from the issues they don't know they are bound in. Forgiveness of our sins is part of the process. But we need to keep in mind that Jesus said many did not want to come to Him (see John 3:19–20).

The answers to life have been given by the One who gives life. The Bible is God's treasure of knowledge, which He has freely given to us, but it has to be studied to gain that knowledge. This man experienced complete deliverance from the prison of darkness in only a moments time. We who read this and understand it can honestly say the man needed the help that Jesus gave him. That man's mind was cleaned up, but not yet renewed. We are instructed in the Word of God to renew our minds once we come to Christ, so that we will experience the process of deliverance.

I have experienced deliverance bit by bit over several years. God chose to deliver me slowly throughout the years. It's been a long, slow process, yet the teaching I've received from Jesus is priceless. Although I wasn't quite in the same shape this man was in, Jesus has done a wonderful work in teaching me, and delivering me from the spiritual chains of darkness that I was in. This is His gift to us. Hallelujah! Philippians, chapter 1, verse 6, tells us that the work Jesus begins in us, He will finish until the day of the Lord. I hold on to this promise.

Another thing we can learn about this situation in these verses is that Jesus can give us this measure of freedom in a moment's time, if He so chooses. But I can testify that when the deliverance is a slow process, the individual can learn how to close the doors of sin in life, and know better how to keep the freedom. Whether it's a quick deliverance, or a slow lengthy one, the results should be the same.

It's worth noting that the presence of Jesus caused the demons to fall and begin to worship (Luke 8:28). In the presence of Jesus the demons were stirred, and had to leave. Jesus is the Word (John 1:14), and the Word is the Bible Scriptures. The Word has the same effect on the evil spirits as does the person of Jesus, because He is the Word. The Word invites the Spirit, and the Spirit brings the Word to life. The Word is very powerful; we are to use it to clean our thoughts, to renew our minds, and repel the evil that wants in.

If you haven't accepted Jesus Christ as your Lord and Savior and would like to do so, don't wait another minute. Jesus knows your situation in life and is desiring that you say yes to Him. He wants to give you a new life in Him, and in His kingdom. If you would like to surrender your life to Jesus and let Him begin to deliver you from the chains of darkness that you are probably not even aware of, pray the prayer below from your heart out loud to God, get a Bible, and read daily. Freedom will come.

Prayer for Salvation

God, I believe that You are the One true God, and that Jesus was
Your Son. I believe that Jesus came into this world and
died on the cross, taking the punishment for my sins. Will You
forgive me for the sins I've committed in my life, come into
my heart, and baptize me with Your Holy Spirit? Today, I surrender
my life to You. Today, I confess Jesus as my Lord and my
Savior. Thank You for hearing me. In Jesus' name I pray, amen.

Printed in the United States
By Bookmasters